FIND THE LATEST WORD ON . . .

QUESTION: SHOULD I USE *AMID* OR *AMIDST?*
ANSWER: EITHER. PREFERRED USAGE IS FOR *AMONG. AMID* AND *AMIDST* ARE PRETENTIOUS . . . MOST OF THE TIME.

QUESTION: CAN YOU HELP ME DISTINGUISH BETWEEN *LIE/LAY/LAID*?
ANSWER: YES. BUT LOOK UP THE ENTRY BECAUSE THERE ARE A WEALTH OF EXAMPLES TO MAKE THE DIFFERENCES CLEAR.

QUESTION: I WAS TOLD BY AN ENGLISH TEACHER TO USE *ALL RIGHT,* NEVER *ALRIGHT.* IS THAT STILL TRUE?
ANSWER: NO. IT IS NOW *ALRIGHT* TO USE EITHER SPELLING.

Times are changing and so is word usage. This wonderfully readable—and very useful—reference work brings you up-to-date, provides clear explanations of recent changes, and helps you understand distinctions with an abundance of examples that are as informative as they are amusing.

WHICH WORD WHEN?
by Paul Heacock

WHICH WORD WHEN?

The Indispensable Dictionary of 1500 Commonly Confused Words

Paul Heacock

A LAUREL BOOK
Published by
Dell Publishing
a division of
Bantam Doubleday Dell Publishing Group, Inc.
666 Fifth Avenue
New York, New York 10103

ISBN: 0-440-20388-0

Printed in the United States of America
Published simultaneously in Canada
July 1989

10 9 8 7 6 5 4 3 2 1
KRI

Acknowledgments

A book of this sort does not simply spring into being fully formed. Several people helped it to take shape along the way, from Sallie Gouverneur, who made me write the original proposal in a way that reflected the book I wanted to write, to Jody Rein, whose demands for excellence upon seeing several sections of the manuscript proved to be more help than hindrance.

Friends, family, and associates provided a number of confusable phrases that they found especially bothersome, which were incorporated in the book. Thanks are due Steve Booth, Paul Groncki, Michelle Tokarczik, and Edna R. Zahn for their contributions.

Special thanks are due Ron Schaumburg, who compiled an extensive list of confusables by canvassing his co-workers in the projects department of Reactive Systems, Inc. Steven A. Neil, the Oscar Acosta of his generation of attorneys, also deserves special mention for tracking down the subtle differences that separate one legalism from another.

And finally, no acknowledgments would be complete without grateful mention of my wife, Carol-June Cassidy, who also contributed to the book, and my daughter, Tyler Cassidy-Heacock; they both lived with a rather unlikable maniac during the final stages of writing this book. Their patience, kindness, and love sustained me; without it, this book would have been impossible.

PAUL HEACOCK
February 1988

Preface

This book is designed to take the confusion out of confusable words and phrases. It was written to provide clear, understandable distinctions between terms that are frequently misunderstood and misused.

Such distinctions are hard to find in other books. *Fowler's Modern English Usage* is the granddaddy of all usage guides; it's a wonderful book, but it is not written in a way that most intelligent users of English can understand. Similarly, many dictionaries provide usage notes, but few provide notes that can be readily comprehended by anyone not holding a Ph.D. in English.

After almost a decade as an editor of other people's prose, it became apparent to me that there was a need for a straightforward, easy-to-use reference book that would allow writers and speakers to determine which word they should use when. The result is *Which Word When?*

This book is not meant to replace a standard dictionary. It should be used along with a standard dictionary to make your selection of the right word a simpler matter than it's been in the past.

How to Use this Book

The way this book works is simple. The words are listed alphabetically. Look up the word you are unsure of; it will either be followed by a main entry consisting of two or more words that are frequently confused with each other, or it will be followed by a cross-reference, telling you where to find the main entry. Listed under each main entry are definitions or explanations of the terms in question. Examples are given to further clarify how each word is used.

The definitions given in this book are not exhaustive. Only those senses that might be confused are included. For instance, in the entry for *endemic/epidemic,* only the adjectival definitions of *epidemic* are given, even though the word is frequently used as a noun. This is because *endemic* is never used as a noun and therefore is unlikely to be confused with the noun *epidemic.*

Similarly, parts of speech are given only for those words that can be used in more than one way and that are likely to be confused when they are. If the part of speech isn't confusable, or different uses of a word aren't confusable, the part of speech isn't given.

Frequent reference is made to formal and informal contexts. For the purposes of this book, formal writing is writing meant to be published in one form or another, whether in book form or as a corporate report; it also includes writing meant to make a strong positive impression, as in letters written asking for a job, and writing that will be examined critically, such as research papers in college. Formal speech refers to instances of public speaking, whether the audience is large or small.

Informal writing and speech are how most people write and speak most of the time. Reports for your boss's use, letters to friends, or comments made in a discussion group are examples of informal (or less formal) contexts. Basically, an informal context is one in which people will pay more attention to what's said than how it's said—as long as how it's said doesn't make the meaning altogether unclear.

Also making frequent appearances in this book are the terms *active verb* and *passive verb.* Rather than getting bogged down in a lot of grammatical gobbledygook, these terms are employed to distinguish the two basic ways a verb can be used. An active verb is one that shows activity on the part of the subject of a sentence. In the sentence *He beat his friend, beat* is an active verb. A passive verb is used to show the results of such activity. In the sentence *His friend was beaten, beaten* is a passive verb. Some verbs can function in both active and passive forms, while others (like *beat)* change a bit depending on whether the active or passive voice is used.

There are undoubtedly words that should be in *Which Word When?* that were not included. If your favorite confusables are not here, send them to me in care of the publisher; with luck, future editions of this book will include them.

P.H.

WHICH WORD WHEN?

a/an Although deciding which to use when is generally simple—*a* goes with nouns beginning with consonants, *an* with those starting in vowels—it becomes a problem when dealing with words that start with *h*'s and *u*'s: Is it "*a* hotel" or "*an* hotel"; "*a* honor" or "*an* honor"; "*a* union" or "*an* union"; and even "*a* eulogy" or "*an* eulogy"? The answer is simply to use *a* with words starting with a consonant sound and *an* with words starting with vowel sounds. So it's "*a* hotel" because *hotel* starts with an *h* sound; "*an* honor" since the first sound is "aah"; a *y* sound dictates that it's "*a* union"; and even though it begins with two vowels, the initial *y* sound makes it "*a* eulogy." This same rule holds true when choosing the article to precede an abbreviation: "*a* member of Parliament" is "*an* MP"

able/capable *see* capable

-able/-ible There is no hard-and-fast rule regarding which suffix should be used. Both turn verbs into adjectives meaning "capable of" <*respectable, defensible*>. When in doubt, look it up

abundance/plethora *see* **plethora**

accept/except Mispronouncing *accept* for *except* has led these two to be confused. To *accept* something or someone means "to receive or respond positively" <I'll be happy to *accept* the job, the boat, the car, and the house>. To *except* someone or something means "to leave out" <When choosing gymnasts, I was usually *excepted*>. *Except* is the right choice in the phrase *except for,* which means "leaving out" <I like her hair *except for* those silver streaks>

accessary/accessory At one time *accessary* was used to describe people who intentionally aided a usually illegal act, while an *accessory* was a subordinate thing. This distinction has all but disappeared, and an *accessory* (now the standard spelling) can be either a criminal's accomplice or a piece of jewelry

accountable/liable/responsible Whether one is *accountable, liable,* or *responsible,* one is in charge and should be able to explain what happened. *Accountable* implies the possibility of some sort of punishment <If someone makes off with the typewriters tonight, you'll be held *accountable*>. Being *liable* means there is probably going to be some sort of legal punishment <No jury would find you *liable* after what you've been through>. Being *responsible* implies that one holds an office or title, or acts like one who does <Being the president makes me *responsible* for their lack of expertise>

acquaintance/acquaintanceship Although many dictionaries list *acquaintanceship* as a noun meaning "someone not very well known"—the same definition given for *acquaintance*—*acquaintanceship* serves no useful purpose other than to substitute a longer, more officious-sounding term for a shorter, clearer, more understandable one. Use *acquaintance*

adventurous/adventuresome/venturous/venturesome All four words are used to describe someone inclined to adventure; it is more common, however, to say that a person is *adventurous* or *venturesome,* and to use *adventuresome* or *venturous* to describe events <an *adventuresome* journey>

adverse/averse *see* **averse**

affect/effect One of the most consistently confused pairs of words around, these two can often, but not always, be told apart by keeping in mind that *affect* is usually used as a verb and *effect* as a noun. *Affect* is the right choice in the senses "to put on, to make a pretense of, to tend toward" <She *affected* the style of Jackie O> <He *affected* grave concern although he couldn't have cared less> or "to influence, move, persuade, or sway" <A Shakespearean drama will *affect* a crowd like no other play>. *Effect* is, on the other hand, used for the meanings "result" <When you take part in such ventures, bankruptcy is often the *effect*>, "influence" <Do you really think eating Twinkies can have such an *effect* on the minds of young people?>, or "impression" <all those piled-up magazines give the *effect* of an intellectual atmosphere>, as well as "personal belongings" when used in the plural <she left some fascinating *effects* when she died>. There are, however, cases where *effect* is used as a verb meaning "to cause or bring about" <How could the president *effect* a treaty with those swine?>. There's also the little-used sense of *affect* as a noun in psychology meaning "something that arouses emotions." In general, though, it's best to keep in mind that something that *affects* you will undoubtedly have an *effect* upon you

afflatus/flatulence *Afflatus* is "divine inspiration" <She prayed for *afflatus* when it came time for final exams>. *Flatulence* is "the effects or symptoms of digestive gas or air" <Once she had farted, her *flatulence* was relieved>. Both stem from the same Latin root, meaning "to blow," but they couldn't be more different in English

afflict/inflict *see* **inflict**

ain't Despite being branded incorrect and unusable by every English teacher you ever had, *ain't* is a word that seems unlikely to go away. It should only be used consciously, when you desire the effect it provides; be aware that what might seem like a "cute" turn of phrase to you may be viewed by others as disgustingly cloying or downright ignorant

allergic/allergenic/hypoallergenic/ nonallergenic People are *allergic* to things; those things that cause the allergic reaction are described as being *allergenic;* things that are less likely to cause an allergic reaction are *hypoallergenic;* those items that cannot cause an allergic reaction are *nonallergenic*

allude/refer To *allude* to something is "to mention indirectly" <In resigning, she alluded to her "past indiscretions," but no one knew what they were>. To *refer* is "to mention directly" <She *referred* to her past indiscretions, defending each as a result of her illness>

allusion/illusion *see* **illusion**

almost/most *see* **most**

almost never/hardly ever *see* **hardly ever**

already/all ready *Already* modifies a verb and means "previously" <Have you *already* accepted a transfer this year?> or "by now" <Finished *already?*>. *All ready* is not a modifier but a phrase that means "every one of us is ready, complete, or prepared" <The crew was *all ready* to get to work despite having little warning>

alright/all right *Alright* has been gaining acceptance as a variant spelling of *all right,* meaning "certainly, yes" or "acceptable, correct." Some sticklers still maintain that the only correct form is as two words, *all right.* But unless you mean "everyone or everything is correct" <When she graded the tests she realized her students were *all right* about the way question three was phrased>, it really is *alright* to use either spelling

alternate/alternative As nouns and adjectives, *alternate* and *alternative* can be used interchangeably to indicate additional possibilities <When the weather is bad, our *alternatives* include chess, checkers, or reading> <The *alternate* destinations are also unlivable>. An *alternate* thing, however, can be one that occurs in turn <*alternate* Thursdays> <*alternate*-side-of-the-street parking>, a sense for which *alternative* is not an alternative

although/though *see* **though**

altogether/all together *Altogether* has several senses, including "completely" <We were *altogether* surprised to see the queen playing hopscotch>, "in total" <The weekend cost us three hundred dollars *altogether*>, "for the most part" <*Altogether* the class of eighty-seven was a major disappointment>, or when used with *the,* "naked" <We found him wandering the neighborhood in the *altogether*>. *All together* means only "all in one place at one time" <Unless you can get the actors *all together* again, the play won't have the same magic it did>

ambivalence Less careful writers and speakers sometimes use *ambivalence* to indicate a lack of concern on someone's part or a dislike for something. It actually means "changing and contradictory feelings" <Your *ambivalence* is infuriating. Make up your mind and either go out with her or don't>

amenable Something or someone can be said to be *amenable* if it is "persuadable" <I'm *amenable* to seeing that movie>, "responsible" <The religious among us are *amenable* to a higher authority>, or "judgeable" <Life-forms are *amenable* to biological tests>. The term should not be used to mean "friendly" or "likable," although it is often misused this way

amid/amidst Both *amid* and *amidst* mean "in the middle of," but both are the sort of highfalutin literary terms best avoided in writing and speech. In most instances it's better to use *among*

among/amongst *Among* and *amongst* are synonyms, but *among* is preferable to *amongst* in most contexts because *amongst* is a term that sounds like the writer is putting on airs. Save *amongst* for use when a snobbish tone is desired for effect

among/between Fanatical quibblers incorrectly maintain that *among* is used to compare more than two items, and *between* is for relations between two things only. But *between* describes any relation of two or more parties that is individual and distinct <negotiations *between* the five front-line nations> <a discussion *between* two opponents and a supporter> <*between* you, me, and the fly on the wall>, while *among* refers to a more general relationship with an unspecified number of others <I wanted to be *among* the French speakers>

amoral/immoral An *amoral* act is one with no regard for morality one way or the other <Our *amoral* life-style allows us to live without judging others>. An *immoral* act is one that is deemed intrinsically wrong <Many believe the war in Vietnam was immoral>

amount/number An *amount* is a general, unspecified, indiscrete quantity <The *amount* of work I have to finish before deadline is staggering>. A *number* refers to specific, countable things, even if the quantity is indefinite <The *number* of manuscript pages I have to finish before deadline is staggering>

amuse/bemuse *see* **bemuse**

an/a *see* **a**

and Everyone knows that *and* is used to join two nouns together <peanut butter *and* jelly>. But many believe it cannot be used at the beginning of a sentence. These people were probably afflicted with an overbearing elementary school teacher. It's okay to use *and* as the first word in a sentence, provided the writer is conscious of the fact that this is a dramatic technique that can be easily overused. It should be used only occasionally. It should be used only to start short sentences. But it can be used this way <*And* that's the truth>

and/or This entry deals not with a choice between *and* and *or* but with the phrase *and/or.* In most contexts, *and/or* is to be avoided. It does serve the purpose of providing a short, easy way of saying "either this or that or both of them together" and has its place in legal and business documents. Still, careless use results in statements like "The batter could get a hit *and/or* a walk," when even a casual baseball observer knows you get one or the other, but never one or the other or both

angel/cherub *see* **cherub**

antagonist/protagonist *see* **protagonist**

anxiously/eagerly *Anxiously* is used when you suffer from anxiety; you're upset and generally unhappy <I *anxiously* await your response to my application>. *Eagerly* implies that you are so looking forward to the event you can hardly wait; you're pleased and restless <I *eagerly* await our weekend together>

anymore/any more Either styling can be used to mean "any longer" or "now, these days," although *anymore* is more common.

ape/monkey/simian *see* **simian**

apprehend/comprehend Both words generally mean "to understand," but *apprehend* has the sense of seeing that something exists <I went to Italy to *apprehend*

Michelangelo's *David*> or understanding at a basic level <to *apprehend* the technique used in Michelangelo's *David*>, while *comprehend* implies grasping the full meaning of something <to *comprehend* Michelangelo's purpose in creating the *David*>

apt/liable/likely *see* **likely**

are/is *see* **is**

arbiter/arbitrator While both terms can refer to a judge empowered to settle a dispute, an *arbiter* is often a final, absolute judge <Hitler was the ultimate *arbiter* of right and wrong in Nazi Germany>, while an *arbitrator* is generally a person chosen by disputing parties to settle an argument <Before my neighbor and I came to blows, we went to an *arbitrator* to determine where the property line really is>

arise/rise *see* **rise**

around/round *see* **round**

as/like *see* **like**

as regards/in regard to/with regard to *see* **in regard to**

Asian/Oriental *see* **Oriental**

assay/essay The verb forms of these two words are essentially the same: "to test, to try, to attempt." However, because the noun sense of *assay* means "an analysis of the quality or composition of an ore, chemical, etc.," many writers confine the verb sense of *assay* to "to test" <I would *assay* that white powder before arresting its possessor> and use *essay* to mean "to attempt, to try"

<Should she *essay* climbing that mountain?>. Most writers don't use either of these words, though; they use *try* or *test*

assure/insure/ensure *see* **ensure**

assume/presume *see* **presume**

atlas/gazetteer *see* **gazetteer**

attorney/barrister/solicitor/lawyer *see* **barrister**

aught/naught *Aught* can mean either "all, anything" or "zero," while *naught* always means "nothing, zero." The "zero" sense of *aught* came from miswriting *a naught* as *an aught.* The best bet is to use *naught* for "zero, nothing" and *aught* for "all." But since it sounds horribly stilted anyway, it is best not to use *aught* at all

authentic/genuine *see* **genuine**

author/write It is symbolic of the vagaries of the English language that the verb *author,* "to be the author of," appeared as long ago as 1596, became obsolete, and has now reemerged as a "new" verb formed from an old noun. Many feel it's a pompous word that serves no real purpose. They believe the word *write* serves quite adequately. While a case might be made for *author* as a verb with the meaning "to be the published author of," it's best not to use *author* as a verb; use *write* instead

avenge/revenge Both verbs are based on *vengeance,* and they are almost synonymous. When a wrong is *avenged,* it means satisfaction is exacted by punishing the wrongdoer <Society was *avenged* for his heinous crimes when he was sentenced to jail>. When a wrong is *revenged,* the wrongdoer is made to suffer the same fate he or she inflicted on the person who was wronged <I'll *revenge* that practical joke by pulling one on her>

avenue/road/street *see* **road**

average/mean/median *see* **mean**

averse/adverse Both of these terms describe opposition. *Averse* usually refers to emotions, as in "having a feeling of repugnance or distaste." *Averse* is usually used with *to* <She's *averse* to spending more>. *Adverse* also means "opposed," but usually refers to circumstances, as in "hostile, unfavorable." *Adverse* can be used without the word *to* <an *adverse* situation>

avert/avoid To *avert* is "to stop something from happening, to turn away" <I shall *avert* my eyes> <Nuclear annihilation must be *averted*>. To *avoid* is "to stay away from" <By remaining on the moon, they avoided nuclear annihilation>

awhile/a while *Awhile* means "for a while." So when the word *for* appears, there should be a space <We'll be visiting for *a while*>, and when the preposition is left out, the space should go too <You'll be in those seats *awhile*>

B

backward/backwards The preferred form for any use is *backward.* When *backward* is used as an adjective the *s* should never be used <a *backward* person>. *Backwards* is acceptable when an adverb meaning "to the back" or "with the back part first" is needed <This train seems to be running *backwards*>

bad/badly When describing someone's physical or emotional state, choose the adverb *bad* <We feel *bad* about your recent loss> <She looks so *bad,* I could cry>. When talking about the extent of such a state with modifiers such as *very* or *so, badly* can be used to mean "severely, strongly, compellingly" <His refusal hurt me so *badly,* I jumped off the bridge>

bail/bale You post *bail* to get someone out of prison. You *bail* water if your boat has sprung a leak. You can put animals in a *bail,* "a pen or other enclosure." A *bail* is one name for the curved handle on a bucket, and for the bar that holds paper in place on a typewriter. But you gotta jump down, turn around, and pick a *bale* ("a closely packed, bound, and wrapped package") of cotton. And *bale* can also mean "anguish, sorrow, woe, evil" <The crowd that had witnessed the execution felt a great *bale*>; this last sense also gives us *baleful,* "sorrowful"

bark/barque A dog may have a *bark* that's worse than its bite, but a ship's captain can command a *bark* or a *barque,* either spelling signifying a ship, usually a three-masted sailing ship

baroque/rococo These two words are related but not quite interchangeable. Both describe architecture, art, literature, or music that is ornate and elaborate. But while the *baroque* tends toward the grotesque and the contrasting, *rococo* indicates the use of elaborate designs to produce a fine, delicate effect. It may help to remember the baroque period in Europe came first, in the late 17th century, and then was refined to become the rococo period in the first half of the 18th century

barrister/solicitor/attorney/lawyer They're all lawyers, "professionals who provide legal advice and representation," but the terms represent different specializations. *Barrister,* "a trial lawyer," and *solicitor,* "a legal agent, representative, or one who prepares cases for trial," are British terms that distinguish different aspects of the legal profession in that country. An *attorney* is "one appointed to conduct business for another or represent another in legal transactions," although an attorney can also plead cases in court. The most encompassing term is *lawyer,* "one authorized to plead cases in courts, give advice, and manage or represent the affairs of others." When Shakespeare wrote, "The first thing we do, let's kill all the lawyers," he was suggesting we get rid of everyone in the profession

basal/basic Both terms mean "essential, fundamental." *Basal* is used in the senses of "minimum necessary for maintaining life in an organism" <The *basal* organs include the heart, lungs, and kidneys> and "used for instructing beginners" <*basal* texts>. *Basic* includes senses dealing with chemistry, "characteristic of a chemical base," and geology, "containing little silica," as well as the more general sense "fundamental"

bathos/pathos *Bathos* can mean "the sudden appearance of the ordinary in lofty material," "an anticlimax," "triteness," or "insincere or overdone pathos; sentimentality." *Pathos,* on the other hand, is "the quality of sadness, pity, or sympathy." *Bathos* elicits smirks; *pathos* evokes sympathy

bay/gulf/strait/sound A *bay* is "a small inlet of the sea or other body of water partly enclosed by land." A *gulf* is "a larger body of water, also enclosed in part by land." A *strait,* however, is "a narrow passageway connecting two large bodies of water." A *sound* is "a long, narrow connecting body of water that is larger than a strait" *see* **sea/ocean**

beauteous/beautiful Both terms are used to describe something as "esthetically pleasing" and are synonymous <The *beauteous* dancers put on a *beautiful* show>

because/since Either of these two can be used to indicate "for the reason that." *Because* is the stronger term, showing a direct link between the occurrences being discussed <I like her *because* she is brainy and beautiful>. *Since* provides a more tenuous link, but indicates a logical connection made by the passage of time <I like her, *since* she has become brainy and beautiful>. When using *since* it's important to be sure there is some sense of time passing or that one thing is the result of the other. If in doubt, *because* is usually the better choice

before/prior to In most cases, *prior to* is just an unnecessarily stuffy way of saying *before* <Let's fool around *prior to* dinner>. *Prior to* is legitimately employed when one event not only precedes another but is necessary or required for the second event <*Prior to* the World Series, two teams must win their league championships>

below/under There is a slight difference in the use of these prepositions, which should be observed by careful writers and speakers. *Below* suggests a comparison between separate, unrelated things <The floor is *below* me> <Jane ranks *below* John in IQ>; *under* implies a much more direct interrelationship between the things being compared <My employee works *under* me> <The cat hides *under* the bed>

bemuse/amuse Perhaps these terms are confused because they sound alike. To *bemuse* is "to stupefy, confuse, bewilder, cause to be preoccupied by deep thought"; to *amuse* is "to entertain humorously, pleasantly, or enjoyably." <I was greatly *bemused* by her suggestion that warfare would *amuse* most people>

benign/malign Another case of two terms being confused because of how they sound. *Benign* is an adjective that means "harmless, gracious, favorable, of a kind and gentle disposition"; it's a very positive thing to say of someone or something. *Malign* can be a verb or an adjective; as an adjective it means "evil in nature, showing intense ill will, virulent" <Norman Bates looked so *benign,* it's hard to believe he could be such a *malign* human being>. In medicine, tumors are often described as either *benign* (harmless) or malignant (tending to grow progressively worse)

benefactor/beneficiary A *benefactor* bestows benefits on others. A *beneficiary* is one of those others who receive the benefits

bereaved/bereft While *bereft* can mean *bereaved,* "suffering from the death of a loved one" <Frankie Valli was *bereaved* by his daughters' deaths>, it can also mean simply "lacking, deprived of some necessity" <I was *bereft* of baseball scores throughout my stay in Ghana>

beside/besides *Beside* can mean *besides,* "except for, in addition to" <We have no one to turn to *besides* you>. *Beside* also can mean "next to, compared with, not pertinent to" <Stand *beside* me> <That's *beside* the point>. It's best to use *besides* when "except for" or "in addition to" are meant, and to save *beside* for meanings it alone has

best/better There is only one *best* <Sadaharu Oh is the *best* professional home-run hitter ever>. If a woman improves on what's been done before, she is doing it *better.* And if she does it *better* than anyone else, she is the *best*

between/among *see* among

bi-/semi- There is simply no avoiding confusion if these words are used. *Semi-* means "twice within a"; a semimonthly publication appears twice a month. Unfortunately *bi-*, while strictly interpreted as "every other," can mean either "every other" or "twice within a"; a bimonthly publication could appear every other month or twice a month. The only reasonable solution is to use *semi-* for "twice within a," *every other* when that's what is meant, and not to use *bi-* at all *see* **by-/bi-**

biannual/biennial More *bi-* problems. Historically speaking, a *biannual* event takes place twice a year and a *biennial* one occurs over the course of two years or once every two years. But the English language changes, meanings change, and a growing minority now uses *biannual* to mean "once every two years." What to do? One option is to never use *biannual,* but that's unreasonable. Another is to make sure the meaning is clear from the context <Our *biannual* report again discusses growth. During the six months since our last report . . .> <This being an even-numbered year, our *biennial* trees will again be bearing fruit>

big/large These two words are usually interchangeable. They differ in the kinds of things they're applied to. *Big* is more frequently applied to physical aspects of people <a *big* nose>, to volume <a *big* noise> <a *big* voice>, and to figurative expressions <*big*hearted> <a *big* fool>. *Large* tends to be used for quantities <a *large* number of items>, for sizes <a *larger* jacket>, and for bulk or mass <*large* office>

bilateral/unilateral/multilateral *Bilateral* means "between two parties" <Britain and France signed a *bilateral* pact>. *Unilateral* means "by one party" <Pakistan's *unilateral* decision to develop nuclear arms was frowned on by its neighbors>. And *multilateral* means "between or among more than two parties" <*Multilateral* talks between the U.S., France, North Vietnam, and South Vietnam went on forever>

bit/bitten The difference between *bit* and *bitten* is the difference between doing the biting and having it done. *Bit* is the active past tense of the verb "to bite" <She *bit* her dog>. *Bitten* is the preferred passive form <Her dog was *bitten*>

bit/byte In the world of computers a *bit* (short for "binary digit") is a single yes-or-no piece of information, recorded as a magnetized spot on a floppy disk or a hole in card or tape. A *byte* is a group of adjacent bits that a computer processes as a single unit. *Bits* are built into *bytes,* which are then made into words, numerals, equations, texts, and so on

bizarre/macabre *see* macabre

blatant/flagrant Both *blatant* and *flagrant* describe acts that are obviously incorrect. *Blatant* acts are "crass, vulgar, noisily offensive" <Belching before the queen is a *blatant* error>. *Flagrant* acts tend to be purposely immoral or illegal <a *flagrant* breach of the treaty> <a *flagrant* flaunting of the standards of her times>

blessed/blest *Blest* is simply an alternate spelling of the verb and adjective *blessed.* They can be used interchangeably

bloc/block A *bloc* is "a group of people, organizations, or countries joined in a common purpose or action" <The Democratic *bloc* tried to stop approval of the president's nominee>. All other senses are covered by *block*

<building *blocks*> <Just put your neck on that *block* while I sharpen my ax> <walk around the *block*>

blond/blonde The differentiation between men with yellowish hair *(blond)* and women with similar hair *(blonde)* is more and more regarded as unnecessary. *Blond* is adequate for both sexes, and avoids the smirking stereotype often implied by *blonde*

bloom/blossom When speaking of plants, *bloom* and *blossom* both describe "a flower or flowers" and "the period of flowering" <The cherry *blossoms* are in *bloom*> <The apple tree is in *blossom*>. There are occasions when convention calls for one over the other, as in cherry *blossoms* (not *blooms*), but in general use they're synonymous

boat/ship *Boat* can mean "ship" and *ship* can mean "boat," but generally a *boat* is "a small vessel, often powered by oars or paddles," and a *ship* is "a large vessel propelled by wind or engines." The distinction is more important to sailors than to linguists

bogey/bogie/bogy/boogey The first three words, all pronounced BUG-ee or BO-gee, can mean "a ghost," "a source of fear or perplexity," or in golf, "one stroke over par on a hole" or "an estimated standard score." *Boogey* is either "rock music," "blues music," or "to dance to such music"

born/borne *Born* deals with birth, either literal or figurative <I was *born* to write dictionaries> <This book was *born* of a desire to make lots of money>. *Borne* is the past participle of *bear,* "to carry" <He had *borne* his station in life with great dignity>

borrow/lend/loan *see* **lend**

bountiful/fulsome *see* **fulsome**

bovine A *bovine* is not just "a cow," but also "an ox." As an adjective, it can refer to any of the qualities associated with oxen and cows

brake/break A *brake* stops a car or a train; the word can also be a verb <I *brake* for cookie monsters>. The other *break* is "a separation, disjoining, disruption, quick move" <There's a *break* in the action> <I hope the *break* heals quickly> <The runner *breaks* for third base>

breath/breathe/breadth *Breath* is a noun meaning "the air inhaled and exhaled" <not a *breath* left in him>. The verb form is *breathe* <air so thick we could hardly *breathe*>. Totally unrelated, yet sometimes confused with respiration, *breadth* is "the measurement from one side to the other, width" <Tell me the cabinet's height, *breadth,* and depth>

briar/brier A tobacco pipe is known as a *briar.* The plant from which a *briar* is carved is a *brier,* as is the woody, thorny plant Br'er Rabbit lived near. To keep things confused, *briar* is an acceptable spelling for *brier;* however, *brier* is incorrect when talking about pipes

bring/take To *bring* something is to move it with the speaker from here to there, "to come with" <I'll *bring* the pie> <*Bring* two pieces of ID> <*Bring* home the bacon>. To *take* something is to move it away from a given place, "to go with" <I'll *take* those tickets> <*Take* it away>

Britain/Briton *Britain* is a place made up of England, Scotland, Northern Ireland and Wales. A *Briton* is a person from Britain

broad/wide Both terms refer to how big something is from side to side. *Broad* is used when nonspecifically indicating that something is fairly large across <a *broad* street> <Linebackers tend to be *broad*-shouldered>. *Wide* is used with actual measurements <eight feet *wide*> or when a thing's horizontal extent is emphasized <The doorway is very *wide*>

brochure/pamphlet *Brochures* and *pamphlets* are both small, printed booklets. Generally speaking, advertising and promotional publications are called *brochures,* while informational and political booklets are referred to as *pamphlets.* But this distinction can be ignored, and frequently is

brook/river/kill/stream/creek *see* **kill**

browse/graze In the sense of eating foliage and herbs, or to eat frequently in small quantities, as animals do when eating foliage, *browse* and *graze* can be used interchangeably. If the desired meaning is "to look over casually," *browse* is the correct choice <I like to *browse* in bookstores, but I generally *graze* only at home>

browse/peruse Both words mean "to read," but the kind of reading indicated by each is vastly different. To *browse* is "to read casually"; to *peruse* means "to read closely and attentively" <You can *browse* when you pick up the newspaper, but your teacher expects you to *peruse* your homework assignments>

brunet/brunette Like *blond/blonde,* there's no real excuse for using *brunette* to distinguish a female with brown hair and *brunet* for a similarly coiffed male. Use *brunet* regardless of the person's sex

bug/tap *see* **tap**

burglary/larceny/theft/robbery These terms are not all interchangeable. *Burglary* is "the unauthorized entry into a building with intent to commit a crime" and applies even if no stealing takes place. *Larceny* is "the illegal taking of another's property" and is equivalent to *theft. Robbery* is larceny done in person with violence or the threat of violence

burger/burgher A *burger* is a sandwich and should not be confused with a *burgher,* who is a resident of a city or a prosperous middle-class citizen

burnt/burned As the past tense of the verb *burn,* either *burned* or *burnt* is okay

by-/bi- These prefixes are quite different in meaning. *By-,* sometimes spelled *bye-,* can mean "out of the way" <*by*pass>, "secondary" <*by*way, *by*product>, or "near, close" <*by*stander>. *Bi-* has to do with two of something, meaning either "two" <*bi*focals>, "occurring twice during" <*bi*weekly>, "occurring in intervals of two" <*bi*centennial>, or "favoring both of two options" <*bi*sexual>

byte/bit *see* **bit**

C

cacao/coco/cocoa *see* **coco**

callous/callus *Callus* is the noun meaning "thickened skin" <She practiced guitar until the *calluses* on her fingers started to bleed>. The verb and adjective forms "to thicken skin" and "thick skinned," whether literal or figurative, are spelled *callous* <Some might call Reagan a *callous* old man>

can/may Strictly speaking, *can* denotes whether or not something is possible <People *can* go to the moon>, while *may* is used to give permission <You *may* leave once the other guests arrive>. In the real world, however, *can* is used for both senses, especially in the negative <We *can't* leave before the other guests arrive> where *mayn't* is too stuffy, pedantic, and old-fashioned

canvas/canvass One paints on a *canvas,* hoists the *canvas* ("sails"), sleeps out of doors in a *canvas* ("a tent"), and, if one's boxing skills aren't sharp, hits the *canvas* during a bout. But the noun or verb dealing with soliciting votes, opinions, subscriptions, and the like is *canvass* <Please *canvass* my constituency on the matter> <Gallup conducted the *canvass* from the fourth through the tenth>

capable/able Both words mean "having the physical, emotional, or mental wherewithal" <He's *capable* of murder> <He's *able* to dance the tarantella>. They are interchangeable

capital/capitol Despite repeated drills since elementary school, many people still have trouble remembering which is which. The *Capitol* is the building in Washington, D.C., in which the U.S. Congress meets; state legislatures similarly meet in buildings known as *capitols.* But the city that is the official seat of government, the accumulated wealth of a person or company, and the uppercase letter are all *capitals,* as are the senses meaning "punishable by death" <a *capital* crime>, "excellent, first rate" <a *capital* suggestion>, "very serious, grave" <a *capital* error>, and "the top of a column"

carat/karet/caret/carrot A *carat* is "a unit of weight for precious stones that equals two hundred milligrams." *Carat* is also a variant spelling of *karat,* "a unit of fineness for gold that equals one twenty-fourth part pure gold" <a forty-*carat* ruby set in a twelve-*karat* gold ring>. A *caret* is "a wedgelike mark used by proofreaders, editors, and writers to indicate where material is to be inserted;" it looks like ^ and, despite the sterling quality of some prose, it has nothing to do with gold or precious stones.

And none of these terms should be confused with Bugs Bunny's favorite food, the *carrot*

careen/career Some nitpickers still maintain that the verb sense "to rush headlong in a reckless, out-of-control manner" can be expressed only by *career* and that *careen* should keep just its nautical sense "to tip to one side." U.S. usage has given *careen* the same sense of wild forward motion, making the two interchangeable <First my car *careened* on the ice, then it *careered* on the packed snow>

carousal/carousel *Carousal* is what one does when out carousing, "a drunken, riotous merryment" <His marathon *carousals* were legend>. It may or may not involve a ride on a *carousel,* which is "a merry-go-round"

carousel/merry-go-round More than one educated friend suggested to the author of this book that the difference between these two be described. There is no difference. Both are rides in which the rider travels in a circle about a fixed point, either powered mechanically on wooden horses or on a small platform that's pushed or pedaled

carrel/carol A *carrel* is "a study nook in a library." It's not where you'd want to be at Christmastime; it would be better to be singing *carols* with friends

casket/coffin *see* **coffin**

cast/caste A *cast* can be many things, including "the actors in a show," "the mold or form in which something is constructed," "a facial expression or particular turn of the eye," "a shade of color," or even "the excrement of an earthworm." But when referring to a rigid hereditary social system, such as that practiced by Hindus, the proper term is *caste*

catholic/Catholic The lowercase version means "liberal; broad in outlook, sympathies, or interests; universal" <She's so *catholic* in her outlook since she traveled overseas>. It's the "universal" sense from which the uppercase *Catholic* stems, since it means "the undivided Christian church of ancient times, or any of the modern churches professing to represent that ancient church, especially the Roman Catholic church" <The pope may be *Catholic,* but he's not especially *catholic* when it comes to sexuality>

cel/cell A *cel* is a specialized term used by animators to describe the transparent sheets of celluloid or plastic on which drawings of the action in an animated film are made; by placing one cel after another over the background illustrations, the illusion of motion is achieved. *Cell* is the proper spelling for "the basic independent structure of life" <*Cells* have membranes and nuclei>, for "a single-room dwelling" <Put her in a *cell* and throw away the key>, for "the basic unit of an organization" <the Communist party *cell*>, and for the portion of the atmosphere that behaves as a unit <If that *cell* develops we'll have a storm>

celebrant/celebrator Both of these words mean "one who celebrates," but a *celebrant* is also "a priest officiating at the Eucharist"

cement/concrete *see* **concrete**

centenary/centennial These two refer to a hundredth anniversary or the marking of a hundred-year period. A *centennial* can also be the celebration in honor of a hundredth anniversary, while the *centenary* is generally just used to mean the anniversary itself

center around/center on Some pedants object to *center around* ("focus or concentrate upon") as an illogical phrase, since a center is a point, not an area around something. This is a silly objection in most contexts because *center around* is an idiomatic expression, and idioms don't have to be logical. However, if formal writing is required, or pedantic readers are expected, use *center on* or *revolve around* instead <The debate *centered on* that hotly discussed topic, marital fidelity>

centigrade/Celsius Two words with but a single scale of measurement represented by each—they're interchangeable. Water boils at one hundred degrees and freezes at zero no matter which term is used. Just remember to capitalize the *C* in *Celsius* and lowercase it in *centigrade*

chantey/shanty *see* **shanty**

check/cheque The British form of *check,* "a written order to a bank to pay money," is *cheque.* In the U.S., the proper form is *check* for all senses other than "a person or thing from Czechoslovakia" (a *Czech*)

cheerful/cheery *Cheery* is a somewhat more intense form of *cheerful,* "in good spirits, ungrudging, promoting cheer," although they are so close in meaning that each can be used for the other

cherub/angel In nontheological use the terms share pretty much the same meaning, "a winged celestial being" or, by extension, "one who shares the attributes of winged celestial beings." But watch your step when using these two in theological circles because, believe it or not, there are nine levels of cute little winged critters; *angel* is the lowest order and *cherub* is second from the top, surpassed only by the seraphim

chide/scold Both words mean "to reprimand or rebuke," and either can be used to describe what might be said to an errant child. *Scold* carries the added connotation of anger on the speaker's part, however, while *chiding* is generally constructive criticism <I *scolded* Tyler after she tried to pull my hair out> <I *chided* her about her constant desire for more cookies>

child/kid *see* **kid**

childish/childlike *Childish* and *childlike* both refer to the qualities of being a child, but in different tones. *Childish* is often used to reproach someone regardless of his age <Stop acting so *childish*>, while *childlike* expresses admiration for those innocent, trustful attitudes children display <Michael Jackson's *childlike* approach to the world>

chili/chilly/Chile The food made with beans and meat and the hot pepper used to make that food are known as *chili.* When lack of warmth is noticed, people say they're *chilly. Chile* is a South American republic

chord/cord A *chord* can be "three or more musical notes sounded together" <three-*chord* rock 'n' roll>, "an emotional response" <struck a *chord*>, "a straight line intersecting two points on a curve," "the outside members of a bridge truss," and "the length from the leading edge to the trailing edge of an airfoil." *Chord* is also an alternate spelling of *cord* in its meaning "a string- or cordlike anatomical structure" <vocal *cord*> <umbilical *cord*>. *Cord* also has the meanings "a rope," "an insulated electrical wire," "an executioner's rope," "a rib on a piece of cloth," "a common feeling or force" <the *cord* that binds us one to the other>, and "a stack of firewood 128 cubic feet in volume"

chute/shoot *see* **shoot**

cite/sight/site *Cite* is a verb meaning "to call upon or quote from an authoritative source; to provide a citation" <Be sure to *cite* your sources>. *Sight* is what you have if you're not blind <The *sighted* are fortunate indeed>. And a *site* is "a place where something exists, is going to exist, or is going to happen" <the *site* of today's exercise>

clench/clinch Both terms have to do with holding or securing things. To *clench* is "to hold tight, clutch" <He *clenched* his mommy's arm>, "to bring together tightly" <*clench* your teeth>, or "to secure a nail or bolt by flattening the end that was driven through something." This last sense of securing a nail is also (and more commonly) expressed by *clinch,* which also carries the senses "to secure a bargain, verdict, or argument" <*clinch* a deal>, "to hold an opponent close while boxing," and "to hold fast or firmly" <They *clinched* in a passionate embrace>

climactic/climatic A *climactic* event is one related to a climax <When the gunfire rang out you knew they'd reached the *climactic* scene>. A *climatic* event has to do with climate and weather <The *climatic* change gave her a cold>

cloth/clothe Material or fabric is known as *cloth.* "To drape or outfit with material or clothing" is to *clothe*

coco/cacao/cocoa *Coco* is another name for "the coconut palm" or its fruit, "the coconut." *Cacao* is the name of the tree and the seeds of the tree used to make chocolate and *cocoa. Cocoa* is a powder made from the roasted kernels of the *cacao.* It can also mean the *cacao* seeds themselves or what's known as "hot chocolate"

coffin/casket Both words describe "a box in which the dead are buried," although a *casket* is sometimes "a fancy coffin"

coherence/coherency These words both stand for "the quality of being consistent and intelligible, as in thought or logic." *Coherency* sounds more highfalutin than *coherence* and is slightly newer, but both have been around for 350 years, so the choice is yours

college/university A *college* is "an undergraduate school or division that grants bachelor's degrees," "a part of a university offering a specific group of courses" <the *college* of liberal arts>, or "a technical or vocational institution" <war *college*>. A *university* is "an institution of higher education made up of an undergraduate division and a graduate division comprised of a graduate school and professional schools"

color/tint/hue *see* **hue**

comical/humorous The more general term is *humorous,* "full of humor," which covers everything that is funny for any reason. *Comical* people or events arouse laughter because of their startling and unexpected nature

common/mutual *see* **mutual**

compare/contrast To *compare* two or more items is "to examine the differences and similarities" <*Compared* with Fowler, this book is less scholarly but covers many of the same terms>. *Compare* can also be used when the similarities alone are being examined. When two or more things are *contrasted,* only their differences are examined <Heacock *contrasts* with Fowler in that Heacock is easier to understand>

compare to/compare with Informally, these two phrases are used interchangeably. In more formal contexts, however, *compare to* should be used when examining similarities, especially in metaphorical senses <His style could be *compared to* a sunset; both reach a pinnacle of beauty just before they're over>. *Compare with* is the correct form for examining both similarities and differences, especially in concrete terms <Carter's nominees can be *compared with* Reagan's and not found wanting>

complacent Often incorrectly used to mean "lazy," *complacent* really means either "self-satisfied" <The Mets became *complacent* after their championship season> or "inclined to please or oblige" <Being a *complacent* brown-nose won't get you in with her>

complement/compliment A *complement* is "a completing part" or "counterpart" <This wine is a perfect *complement* to chicken>. It is not the word to use for "a flattering, respectful, or admiring remark," which is a *compliment* <He'll take any remark you make about his work as a *compliment*>. This distinction is easy to remember because *complement* has the *e* of complete and the meaning of "a completing part"

complete/replete *see* **replete**

comprehend/apprehend *see* **apprehend**

comprehensive/comprehensible In addition to meaning "inclusive" or "all inclusive," *comprehensive* can also mean "capable of understanding well or readily" <He is *comprehensive* of foreign languages>. It is not interchangeable with *comprehensible,* "understandable, intelligible" <Her *comprehensive* grasp of mathematics makes her theorems quite *comprehensible*>

comprise/compose Despite two hundred years of synonymous usage, some purists insist on using *comprise* to describe the whole with the meaning "to include" <The team *comprises* twenty-four players> and *compose* to describe the parts, meaning "to make up" <Twenty-four players *compose* the team>. The differentiation is hard to understand and seems to be slowly dying, but if your audience *comprises* picky readers, it's better to use *compose* or *make up* when the subject is the parts of a whole
see **include/comprise**

compulsory/mandatory *see* **mandatory**

concrete/cement *Cement* is one ingredient, mixed with sand or gravel and water, that goes into making *concrete,* "a hard, strong building material." It's likely that decades or centuries of confusion have led to the now quite acceptable use of *cement* to mean "concrete"

conduction/convection *see* **convection**

confident/confidant/confidante *Confident* is an adjective meaning "self-assured" <I'm *confident* I can get my work finished on time>. *Confidant* means "one to whom secrets are entrusted," as does *confidante,* although the version with the *e* is "especially a woman." Since gender isn't as important in English as it is in French, which is the source of this term, *confidante* may as well be discarded as a sexist term

connote/denote To *connote* is "to imply in addition to the exact meaning" <Conner's death could have *connoted* the end of the program>. *Denote* means "to designate, mean, announce" <Yellow lights *denote* a need for caution>

conscience/conscious/conscientious In modern times, *conscience* means "the sense of the goodness or badness of one's own actions or thoughts" <Richard Speck's *conscience* ought to bother him the rest of his life>. *Conscientious* means "governed by conscience, scrupulous" <a *conscientious* student>. *Conscious* means "awake," "personally felt," "noticing with a degree of controlled thought," or "aware." Confusion of these terms is not surprising, since one sense of *conscience* is "conscientiousness," and another, archaic meaning is "consciousness," but each should be used only in the senses outlined above

consensus/consensus of opinion The meanings of *consensus* are "unanimity," "collective opinion," and "the judgment agreed to by most of those concerned," which allows *consensus* to stand for complete agreement or majority agreement within a group. Some feel *consensus of opinion* to be a redundancy, and in the sense "collective opinion" it is, but in the sense "unanimity" it is not. Still, to avoid having nits picked, it's best not to use the phrase in formal usage

consequential This term can mean "secondary, indirect" <The *consequential* impact of yesterday's decision won't affect many people until next year>, "consequent, following as a result of" <In view of his actions, the *consequential* decision was inevitable>, or "important" <a most *consequential* person>. This last sense is frowned upon by some grammarians but has been used for centuries with no ill effects

construe/understand To *construe* is "to analyze or interpret the meaning of" <Diplomats *construe* Iran's posturing as threatening>. To *understand* is "to comprehend, accept, or know" <I can't *understand* how you could think my actions were offensive>. *Understanding* can occur in a number of ways—intuitive, deductive, through divine instigation—while *construing* an act or event requires deductive, analytic reasoning

contemptible/contemptuous The adjective that describes others as "worthy of disdain" is *contemptible* <you *contemptible* lout>, while the one that expresses feelings or expressions of contempt is *contemptuous* <She gave him a withering, *contemptuous* look>

continual/continuous Although nearly synonymous, something is considered *continual* if it goes on uninterrupted forever, while a *continuous* event has a beginning and an end with no stops in between

continuance/continuation Both terms can be used to mean "the act or fact of continuing." *Continuance* also refers to the duration of time for which something occurs <her brief *continuance* in professional basketball> or a postponement of court proceedings to a future day. *Continuation* has to do with prolonging something <the *con-*

tinuation of her basketball career long past her prime> or picking it up again where it's been left off <And now, the *continuation* of our story>

contrast/compare *see* **compare**

convection/conduction With the advent of tabletop ovens, these two terms have come into greater use and have been more frequently confused. *Convection* is "the transfer of heat by a circulatory motion as a result of differing densities and the action of gravity." *Conduction* is "the transmission of heat by means of a conductor." In plain English, *convection* uses air to heat and *conduction* uses coils or other heat sources. And in senses not having to do with heat, *conduction* and *convection* both mean "the act of conveying" <She supervises the *conduction* of tourists to the landmarks>

convince/persuade Both terms mean "to bring to a belief by argument." Grammarians have long insisted that only *persuade* can be followed by *to* <I *persuaded* him to undress>, while *convince* can take *of* or *that* but not *to* <*convinced* of the fact> <*convinced* that it wouldn't happen>. This distinction is so rapidly falling by the wayside it can be ignored in most circumstances <I *convinced* him to undress>

copy/Xerox/photocopy *see* **Xerox**

cord/chord *see* **chord**

corporal/corporeal A *corporal* can be "a cloth used in celebrating the Eucharist" or "a noncommissioned military officer"; as an adjective it can mean "of the body" <*Corporal* warts may be ugly, but they're generally harmless>. *Corporeal* things are those "of a material nature;

nonspiritual; substantial" <She's a *corporeal* woman, uninhibited by religious notions>

corporation/firm *see* **firm**

couch/sofa A *sofa* can be "a couch," and a *couch* can be "a sofa." A *couch* is "a long piece of furniture, usually upholstered and often with a back, on which one can sit or recline." A *sofa* usually has arms and a back, and can often be converted into a bed. To be safe, call a piece of furniture like this whatever the manufacturer says it should be called; if you don't know what the manufacturer calls it, either word can be used

council/counsel/consul A *council* is a group of people assembled for consultation, advice, or discussion; it can be "a legislative body, an administrative body, an executive body, or an advisory group" <The *council* met in a closed session>. *Counsel* can be "advice, a policy, or an act of deliberation" or "a lawyer or consultant" <The *counsel* from my *counsel* is to not answer these questions>. A *consul* is "an appointed representative of a foreign country" <I'd like you to meet the Brazilian *consul*>

crazy/mad *see* **mad**

creek/brook/river/kill/stream *see* **kill**

cretin/mongoloid *see* **mongoloid**

criteria/criterion *Criteria* is the plural form of *criterion,* "a standard on which a judgment is based" <What are my *criteria?* I have only one, and that *criterion* is greed>. It is absolutely incorrect to use such formulations as "a criteria" or "the one criteria"

cue/queue *see* queue

curriculum vitae/resume *see* resume

curse/epithet *see* epithet

cyclone/tornado *see* tornado

dam/damn To *dam* something is "to block or restrain with a barrier" <*Dam* that trickle before it becomes a flood>. To *damn* someone or something is "to condemn to hell; to curse" <*damn* your stupidity>. Some writers have used *dam* when *damn* is intended, apparently to appear less vulgar, but this use is incorrect

data/datum If we all spoke Latin, we would use *datum* to mean "a single piece of information" and *data* for the plural "factual information, such as statistics or numerical quantities." In American English in the late twentieth century, however, *data* is more and more being used in both singular <The *data* is insufficient> and plural <These *data* are insufficient> constructions. A sizable minority of sticklers will disagree, but the singular form is acceptable

debacle This word has grown to encompass meanings it did not originally have. While still having the senses "the breakup of ice in a river" and "a rout, as of an army," it has also taken on the more general meanings "a large-scale disaster" and "a fiasco or failure" <This party was a *debacle*>

debark/disembark *Debark* can be used to mean "to remove from a ship" or "to leave a ship or other vehicle"; it also has the sense "to remove bark from" <Let's *debark* from this car, go into the forest, and *debark* some spruce>. *Disembark* is used only in the sense of leaving a ship or other vehicle

debris/garbage/trash All three terms have to do with waste material but in different senses. *Debris* is "the remains of something broken," "rubble," or in geological terms, "an accumulation of rock fragments." *Garbage* can mean "food waste," "unwanted, useless, or worthless material," or "nonsense." *Trash* means "waste" and also has the meanings "nonsense" and "worthless material," in addition to "inferior writing or artistic items," "something, such as plant trimmings, broken off to be discarded" and "a contemptible person"

decriminalize/legalize When something such as marijuana possession is *decriminalized,* it means such possession is regulated but no longer banned completely. If it were to be *legalized,* possession would not be regulated; it would be approved by the authorities

defective/deficient *Defective* and *deficient* both mean "falling below a standard or norm," although *defective* has to do more with being faulty or lacking a physical quality <a *defective* computer> while *deficient* describes a lack of completeness <mentally *deficient*> <*deficient* resources>

defensible/defendable Both words mean "capable of being defended" and are interchangeable

definite/definitive Although they both deal with precise and explicit limits, *definite* is less absolute than *definitive.* A *definite* solution is one that is clearly explained and agreed upon. A *definitive* solution has these qualities, but is also one that is final and unalterable

delegation/legation *see* **legation**

delimit/limit *see* **limit**

delusion/illusion A *delusion* is "an act of deceiving" <the president's *delusion* of the public in failing to invoke the War Powers Act>, "the state of being deceived," "a false belief held despite contrary evidence" <the failing student's *delusion* that she's academically superior>, or "a false psychotic belief" <*delusions* of grandeur>. An *illusion* is nowhere near as damaging or debilitating, and is usually corrected when contrary evidence is presented; it's "a misleading visual perception" <the *illusion* of motion>, "something that is intellectually deceptive" <Haig gave the *illusion* of being in charge>, or "the state of being intellectually deceived" <I was under the *illusion* that magic was real> *see* **illusion/allusion**

demagogue/ideologue *see* **ideologue**

demon/devil A *demon* is "an evil spirit," "an undesirable emotion or trait" <the *demon* of cigar smoking>, or "someone with a great deal of determination" <a *demon* for exercise>. A *devil* is "the Judeo-Christian personification of supreme evil," "a fiend" <Tyler can be a real *devil* when she doesn't get a nap>, "an energetic and reckless person" <Anna can be quite a *devil* when she's

well rested>, "a person" <you lucky *devil*>, or, synonymous with *demon,* "an evil spirit" <Hold your breath near the graveyard or the *devils* will get you>

demur Some confuse this word with *defer,* others think it means "to mumble," but in reality *demur* can be used as a verb meaning "to object" <The student *demurred* at the assignment> or, less often, "to hesitate," and as a noun meaning "hesitation" or "objection" <He followed orders without *demur*>

denote/connote *see* **connote**

deprecate/depreciate These verbs are synonymous in the senses "to lower the value of" <Our property has *depreciated*> and "to disparage" <Don't *deprecate* your own worth>. *Deprecate* carries the additional meaning "to express mild disapproval of" <She *deprecated* her children's bad behavior>

desegregate/integrate *see* **integrate**

desert/dessert A *desert* is "an arid piece of land." A *dessert* is "a sweet dish eaten at the end of a meal"

detached/unattached *see* **unattached**

diagnosis/prognosis A *diagnosis* is what's commonly referred to as "a medical examination," "the art of identifying diseases through such examinations," or "the opinion derived from such an examination" <My *diagnosis* of your husband leads me to the *diagnosis* that he needs help>. A *prognosis,* which can be based on a medical exam, is "the likeliness of recovery from an illness," "a prediction of the probable course of a disease," or "a forecast"—in common parlance, "the outlook" <The *prognosis* for a lovesick woman is not good>

diarrhea/diurectic *see* **diuretic**

dice/die Several leading dictionaries insist that *dice* is only acceptable as the plural form of *die,* "a small cube marked with dots on each side ranging from one to six." In spoken English, though, and to a lesser extent in writing, *dice* has become fairly acceptable in the sense "one or more dice" <A one came up on one *dice* and a six on the other>

different from/different than There was a time when *different from* was the only acceptable way of phrasing a comparison of dissimilarity, even when the result was wordy or awkward <Things are *different from* the way I remember them being>. *Different than* is gaining acceptance, however, especially when followed by a clause <*different than* what had been expected>

dinner/supper *Dinner* is "the main meal of the day," whether taken in the early afternoon or in the evening. "The evening meal" is *supper,* especially if the main meal was eaten at lunchtime or if the evening meal is a social affair <a round-robin *supper*>

disc/disk Computers employ floppy *disks.* Audiophiles have started buying compact *disc* players, but many hold on to their old *discs,* "phonograph records." Truly modern electronics buffs also have *discs* to use with their videodisc players. Farmers use *disc* harrows to till the soil. The preferences are set by the industries that produce these various disks or discs, and lexicographers have generally not pushed one variant over the other in these cases. But the preferred spelling for most other senses is *disk* <slipped *disk*> <The moon was a silvery *disk*><She flipped the Frisbee but the *disk* went the other way>

discrete/discreet A *discrete* entity is one that is "separate, distinct" <The *discrete* parts are then assembled>. A *discreet* entity is one that is "modest, respectful of propriety" <Be *discreet* whenever he's nearby>

disembark/debark *see* **debark**

disinterested/uninterested Some stern grammarians say *disinterested* can only mean "unbiased"; however, it has meant "not interested" and "no longer interested" since the fifteenth century. It continues to have both meanings, while *uninterested* means "indifferent" or "without a financial stake or interest" <I'm *uninterested* in wild debauches these days>

disposal/disposition Either *disposal* or *disposition* can be used in the senses "a particular arrangement or ordering of things" <the artful *disposal* of the vases>, "a particular way of attending to something" <your *disposition* of the staff>, "the transfer of something to someone else" <*disposal* of the estate>, "the getting rid of something" <*disposition* of the wrecked car>, or "the liberty to deal with something as one chooses" <at your *disposal*>. But when discussing someone's "inclination, temperament, or tendency," the proper term is *disposition*

dissemble/disassemble To *dissemble* is "to hide the true nature of" <*dissemble* amusement behind a stern countenance>, or "to simulate" <*dissemble* a drunken bum>. To *disassemble,* despite the similar spelling, is "to take apart," "to come apart," or "to scatter" <Don't try to *disassemble* it without a manual>

dissoluble/dissolvable Either of these words can be used to mean "capable of being dissolved" <The wicked old witch was *dissoluble*>

distinct/distinctive *Distinct* is used to show that something is "separate" <Hundreds of cars were parked in the lot below, each one *distinct*>, whereas *distinctive* serves to show it is "unique, distinguishing" <His car has a *distinctive* stripe>. *Distinct* can also mean "clear" <a *distinct* sign>, "unquestionable" <a *distinct* chance of winning>, or "unlike" <*distinct* from the others>. *Distinctive* has the added sense of "characteristic" <a *distinctive* walk>

diuretic/diarrhea Both terms deal with bodily wastes, but otherwise have little in common. A *diuretic* substance is one that is "likely to increase urination" <A quantity of beer will have a *diuretic* effect>. *Diarrhea* is "loose excrement"

diurnal/nocturnal *Diurnal* has to do with the daytime, as in "occurring every day" <a *diurnal* job> or "active in the daytime" <a *diurnal* creature>. *Nocturnal* is the opposite, something that is "occurring nightly" <*nocturnal* news programs> or "active at night" <*nocturnal* life-style>

dived/dove Both are correct for the past tense of *dive. Dived* is somewhat more common in written English in most of the U.S., although in the northern U.S. and Canada *dove* is the standard form, especially in speech

dock/jetty/pier/wharf In the sense of "a structure built in the water for loading and unloading materials and people," all four words are interchangeable, although a *wharf* is usually supported by wooden piles and a *pier* is held up by masonry. A *pier* is also usually set at a right angle to the shore. These differentiations have, to a great extent, been blurred by the passage of time and the dwindling use of water transport. *Jetty* and *pier* are also used to mean "a breakwater," while a *dock* can also be "the waterway in which ships sit while loading or unloading"

domesday/doomsday *Domesday* is the Middle English version of *doomsday,* "the (or a) judgment day," that survives primarily in the phrase *Domesday Book,* which is a census record from eleventh-century England. Except for special effect, use *doomsday*

doubtless/undoubtedly These words are interchangeable adverbs meaning "without doubt" or "probably" <It is *doubtless* an activity that would cause injury>

douse/dowse *Dowse* can be a variant spelling of *douse,* "to drench with water or extinguish" <*Douse* the fire>. *Dowse* is also a verb meaning "to use a divining rod to find water"

draft/draught *Draught* is simply the British spelling of *draft* in any of its senses, from "an act of drinking or inhaling" and "a team of animals that pull loads" to "an air current" and "a preliminary sketch." In the U.S., it's best to use *draft*

drank/drunk *Drank* is simply the active past tense of *drink* <I *drank* all the water>. *Drunk* was once acceptable in this sense but is now used for the passive past tense

<The soda was all *drunk* before she arrived>, as an adjective <We were *drunk*>, or as a noun <that crazy old *drunk*>

dribble/drivel A *dribble* is "a small trickle, especially of saliva," "a tiny bit of something," or "the act of bouncing a ball with one hand." *Drivel* can also be "a small trickle of saliva," but it has the quite separate meaning "nonsense" <What kind of *drivel* is that fool telling us now?>

driven/drove Both past tenses of the verb "to drive," they differ in that *drove* is an action taken by the subject of the sentence <We *drove* to the store> while *driven* is passive, something that happens to the subject <She was *driven* to murder by his slovenly habits>

droll Mistaken senses include "dry," "boring," "stuffy," and, somewhat closer to the mark, "dryly humorous." None of these is what *droll* actually means. When something is *droll* it is "of an amusing, humorous, or entertainingly peculiar quality" <Her *droll* stories sometimes begin quite oddly, but they always leave me laughing>

drunk/drunken Both words are adjectives meaning "in a state of having had too much to drink." Good usage requires *drunk* when the noun and adjective are separated by a verb <We got *drunk*>, but when the adjective precedes the noun it should be *drunken* <a *drunken* driver> <the *drunken* old fool>

dust/lint *see* **lint**

duty/tax A *duty* is generally used to mean "a tax levied by a government on imports," while a *tax* can be any sort of "fee or levy imposed by a government on people or property"

dwelling/house/home A *dwelling* is "a shelter in which people live," and can refer to an apartment, a building, or some other sort of shelter. A *house* is "a building in which one or a few families live." And a *home* is "one's own place of residence" <This tent is our *dwelling.* It may not be a real *house,* but we consider it *home*>

dyeing/dying *Dyeing* is "coloring or staining with dye" <the *dyeing* employed in creating Kente cloth>. *Dying* is "stopping life" <*dying* of cancer>, "willing to or as though willing to stop life" <*dying* to get in there>, or "at the end of life" <*dying* words>

each other/one another *Each other* is used more often when there are only two subjects <The pitcher and the batter eyed *each other*>. *One another* more frequently appears when three or more people are involved <The five of them fight constantly with *one another*>. But the terms can be used interchangeably and have been for hundreds of years

eagerly/anxiously *see* **anxiously**

earthly/earthy *Earthly* has a connotation of "nonspiritual" in such meanings as "of the earth" <our *earthly* troubles> and "possible" <no *earthly* reason>. *Earthy,* on the other hand, simply means "of earth or dirt" <the *earthy* smell>, "practical" <an *earthy* approach>, or "crude; uninhibited" <an *earthy* woman who belches when she feels like it>

economic/economical These words can be used synonymously to mean "thrifty" <an *economic* vacation> <an *economical* vacation>. *Economic* also means "of or pertaining to an economy or economics" <an *economic* nightmare> or "profitable" <Pet rocks were an *economic* windfall for someone>

effect/affect *see* **affect**

effete Spiro Agnew, disgraced vice president, introduced this word to a broad audience in the early nineteen seventies, but many who heard it found its meaning unclear. The sense he intended was no doubt "decadent, self-absorbed" <*effete* snobs of the radical left>. Other senses include "worn out," "outmoded," or "no longer fertile"

efficacious/efficient/effective These three words have close but separate meanings. *Efficacious* means "able to have a desired effect, especially by virtue of some special, inherent quality" <Reagan's grandfatherly tone of voice makes him an *efficacious* speaker>. *Efficient* means "able to have a desired effect, especially with little waste" <Giving each of my students the same information separately is not an *efficient* use of time>. *Effective* means simply "able to have a desired effect"

e.g./i.e. Both terms are Latin, and both are used to elaborate on a given point, but they are not interchangeable; *e.g.* is short for *"exempli gratia"* and *i.e.* stands for *"id est."* When a concrete example is introduced, and the meaning is "for example," the proper term is *e.g.* <They built highways, *e.g.,* the Massachusetts Turnpike and the New York State Thruway>. When the phrase that follows elaborates, and the meaning is "that is," the right choice is *i.e.* <the truly poor, *i.e.,* those earning less than five thousand dollars<

egregious/outstanding/exceptional All three words have to do with things beyond the normal or average, but in different senses. *Egregious* means "notably bad" <an *egregious* lapse of judgment>. *Outstanding* means "conspicuous; notably distinguished" <an *outstanding* effort that fell short>. *Exceptional* can be either "superior" or, when describing intelligence or ability, "above or below average" <Both are *exceptional* students, but one needs tutoring while the other could be a tutor>; in this last sense, *exceptional* could be replaced by either *egregious* or *outstanding*

either . . . is/ . . . are Using a plural verb with *either* is a common error. It takes a singular verb <*Either* she or I *am*>. Because there are two subjects, this confusion is easy to understand. But reconstructing the phrases makes this rule clearer <*Either* she *is* or I *am*>. The same rule applies to *neither* as well <*Neither* Fred *reads* nor his uncle *reads*>

élan/style Some dictionaries suggest that *élan* and *style* can be synonymous, but this remains a point of some debate. *Style* has the sense of "graceful or beautiful manners or attitude" <handles herself with *style*>. *Élan* is "vigorous enthusiasm" <mustered a great deal of *élan* for one just out of bed>, although some maintain it, too, can be used to mean "graceful manners." To avoid the appearance of misuse, it's best to employ *élan* only to mean "vigorous enthusiasm"

elder/older Both words mean "of a greater age." The adjective *elder* is generally used to refer only to people, especially people in one's own family <my *elder* brother>. *Older* is most often employed in reference to things rather than people <*Older* computers work just as well>. The same distinction applies to *eldest* and *oldest*

electric/electrical/electronic Both *electric* and *electrical* refer to things "powered or operated by electricity" <*electric* typewriter> <*electrical* drill>. *Electronic* devices are those "working on the principles of the movement of electrons" <*electronic* audio amplifiers, not vacuum-tube models>

elemental/elementary *Elemental* and *elementary* can both be used to mean "fundamental," "rudimentary," or "having to do with the natural elements." *Elemental* can also mean "of or pertaining to chemical elements" and "inherent" <an *elemental* sense of direction>, while *elementary* has the added sense of "having to do with an elementary school" <the *elementary* curriculum>

elusive/illusive That which is *elusive* is "physically hard to grasp," "hard to understand" <Math is an *elusive* subject>, or "hard to identify." That which is *illusive* is "deceptive" or "based on an illusion" <The candidate's portrayal in his TV ads was *illusive*> *see* **illusion/allusion**

emigrate/immigrate Those who *emigrate* leave a country to live elsewhere. Those who *immigrate* enter a country to take up residence. For those who like mnemonics, remember that *emigrate* is "to *e*xit" and *immigrate* is "to come *i*nto." The noun forms *emigrant* and *immigrant* are similarly "one who leaves a country" and "one who enters a country"

eminent/imminent Something that's *eminent* stands out, projects, or in the sense used to describe people, is "displaying superior qualities" <an *eminent* scholar>. Something that's *imminent* is about to happen <his *imminent* demise>

emotive/emotional These terms can be interchanged when the meaning is "of or relating to emotions" <an *emotive* disturbance> <an *emotional* display>. *Emotive* also has the sense of "able to express emotion or excite emotion in others" <an *emotive* actor>. *Emotional* has the meanings "stirred by emotion," "arousing emotion in oneself." A depressingly *emotional* man is one who cries all the time; a depressingly *emotive* man is one who makes everyone else cry all the time

empathy/sympathy *Empathy* is "the experience of another's feelings or experiences" <Being a doctor myself, I have great *empathy* for other doctors whose patients die>. *Sympathy* is "the understanding of another's feelings or experiences" <Although my parents are still alive, I have great *sympathy* for those whose parents have died>. *Empathy* involves a direct sharing of how someone else feels, whereas *sympathy* involves an appreciation for how someone feels without experiencing that feeling

endeavor/try Both words involve making attempts at accomplishing something. *Try* means simply "to make an attempt," but *endeavor* is "to make an earnest effort at accomplishing something." Use of *endeavor* should be restricted to instances of serious, concerted effort <I will *endeavor* to obtain an A in your course> <I'll *try* to make it to the dance Friday>

endemic/epidemic Because both terms have some medical senses, they are sometimes confused. *Endemic* means "peculiar or native to a given place or population" <Malaria is *endemic* to tropical climes>. *Epidemic* is "spreading rapidly within a given place or among a given population" <AIDS became *epidemic* within the gay community>, and this adjectival sense of *epidemic* is sometimes mistakenly thought to be conveyed by *endemic*

endure/survive In their confusable senses, *survive* and *endure* both mean "to continue to exist or be alive" <*survive* the arctic temperatures> <temples that *endure* for thousands of years>. *Endure* can also mean "to remain steadfast despite opposition" <friendship that can *endure* criticism> or "to carry on despite hardship" <Our tour *endured* forty days of rain>, senses for which *survive* is not appropriate in formal usage, although it is frequently used this way in less formal contexts

enervate/energize These two sound similar but are opposite in meaning. To *enervate* is "to dissipate, reduce, or lessen" <The job emotionally *enervated* him to the point where he didn't care>, whereas *energize* means "to enliven, invigorate" <*energize* the sales staff so they actually sell something>

enliven/liven *see* **liven**

ennui The only definition of *ennui* is "boredom." It should not be used in any other sense, although it often is given meanings like "stylishness" or "sophistication." It is pronounced "on-WEE"

enormity/enormousness For about two hundred years, *enormity* has been used in one sense to mean "immensity, hugeness" <The *enormity* of the problem is such that we must throw money at it>. Many grammarians, however, insist on *enormousness* for this meaning. Either word is correct. Arguments can be avoided altogether, though, by using *immensity* instead

enquire/inquire *Enquire* is simply a variant spelling of *inquire,* "to ask"; either is acceptable

ensure/assure/insure All three terms mean "to make sure," and they are broadly interchangeable. *Assure* has the additional sense of "to put someone at ease about something" <I *assure* you he's all right>. *Insure* is the word that means "to guarantee against loss of life, health, or property" <Lloyd's will *insure* my hands for a million bucks>. *Ensure* has no other meanings; it simply means "to make sure"

enthuse The verb *enthuse,* meaning "to show enthusiasm" or "to make enthusiastic," was formed from the noun *enthusiasm* about 150 years ago, but it is still frowned upon by careful and formal writers. In some contexts it is acceptable, notably in journalism, letter writing, and popular works. But it is an unpleasant word that lacks the euphony of its alternatives <She *enthused* about her work> <She *waxed enthusiastic* about her work>

entitle/title As verbs meaning "to give a title to," *entitle* and *title* are interchangeable <I thought I'd *entitle* my next book *A Bozo's Delight,* but my editor thinks it would be better to *title* it *The Wandering Fool*>

entomology/etymology Both have to do with the little things in life, but *entomology* is "the study of insects" and *etymology* is "the study of the history of words"

epicure/gastronome/gourmet All three terms describe "a person who is knowledgeable about and enjoys good food and drink." An *epicure* is overly careful about what's being eaten and drunk and takes great enjoyment in consuming it. A *gastronome* will know about the history and cultural importance of what's being eaten. And a *gourmet* tends to be discriminating and to enjoy knowing about the subtleties of what's being consumed. But these distinctions are not universally applied, so in general use, all three are synonyms *see* **gourmet/gourmand**

epigram/epigraph/epithet An *epigram* is "a terse, witty, or wise saying" <"Drunk driving can kill a friendship" is an *epigram* of our times>. An *epigraph* is "a quotation that appears at the beginning of a literary work designed to set the tone for what follows" <Dictionaries generally do not include an *epigraph*>. An *epithet* is "a word or phrase that characterizes or disparages something or someone" <"Scum" is the *epithet* she chose to describe her date>

epithet/epitaph As described in the preceding entry, an *epithet* is "a word or phrase that characterizes or disparages something or someone" <"Mr. Fun" is our *epithet* for Billy Martin>. An *epitaph* is "an inscription on a tombstone" or "a brief commemorative statement" <I'd like my *epitaph* to read I TOLD YOU I WAS SICK>

epithet/curse In one sense, *epithet* and *curse* are similar, but the two terms really aren't interchangeable. An *epithet* can be disparaging (see above) and carries a sense of words that characterize someone. *Curses* are "prayers for harm or invocations of evil" or "abusive profanity," but they don't generally describe the person being cursed <a *curse* like "I wish God would strike you dead">

equivalence/equivalency Although either word can be used to mean "approximate equality," *equivalence* is the more common choice. *Equivalency* is employed to describe a high-school diploma earned after dropping out

equivalent/equal *Equivalent* means "approximately the same" <Use butter or an *equivalent* fat>. *Equal* is "exactly the same" <Use a cup of milk or an *equal* amount of water>

ere/err *Ere* is a word not many can use without sounding ridiculous. It means "before" <*ere* he drove out of sight>, and *before* would be a better choice in most contexts. It should not be confused with *err,* a more common word meaning "to make a mistake" <*err* on the side of caution>

erstwhile Although frequently thought to have many other meanings, such as "honored" or "absent," *erstwhile* serves only as an adjective meaning "former" <an *erstwhile* director> and as an adverb meaning "formerly" <We were *erstwhile* discussing that topic>

esoteric/exotic *see* **exotic**

especial/special *Special* is the general term when the meaning is simply "not ordinary" <a *special* day>. When the sense is "extremely unordinary; preeminent; distinctive and unusually significant," the word to use is *especial* <an *especial* decision affecting the whole world>. Because *special* covers the same senses in a more general way, it, too, can be used when *especial* would be correct.

Use *especial* to add emphasis to the unusual nature of what's being described

especially/specially Like the adjective forms in the preceding entry, the adverbs *especially* and *specially* are very close in meaning. As an adverb, however, *specially* doesn't cover quite as much territory, with the result being a clearer-cut use for each. *Especially* is used when the meaning is "to an exceptional degree" or "particularly" <at this *especially* trying moment in history>. *Specially* means "for one particular purpose" <*specially* designed shoes>

essay/assay *see* **assay**

essentially/substantially *Essentially* means "in essence; at a basic or ultimate level" <She is *essentially* stupid>. *Substantially* can also mean "at a basic level" <She is *substantially* stupid> or can have the sense of "considerably; importantly" <His attitudes have changed *substantially*>

etc. This abbreviation for *et cetera* means "and other things of the same sort" or "and so on." The main problem incurred in using it is not confusion about these meanings but its inappropriateness in many contexts. *Etc.* should never be used to end a list that begins with *such as* because *such as* shows a reader that the list is incomplete <animals such as birds, bears, *etc.*>. Careful writers avoid it altogether, since in most cases it's used to mean "and a bunch of other stuff I don't think is particularly important," and if it's not particularly important, it shouldn't be mentioned at all

ethical/moral *Ethical* and *moral* are both adjectives that are loosely interchangeable to describe what's good as opposed to what's bad. The essential difference between them is that *ethical* has to do with professional standards or what is thought to be good by a group <Professors must be *ethical* in dealing with students of the opposite sex>, while *moral* most often has to do with an individual's judgments <The *moral* choice for many people is to oppose nuclear weapons>. *Moral* also applies to what is considered good by organized religions or by society at large

etymology/entomology *see* **entomology**

evangelical/fundamentalist In one sense, *evangelical* (with or without a capital *e*) means "Protestant"; in another sense it means "being in agreement with the Christian gospels"; in yet another, it's "believing in salvation obtained through faith, Scriptural study, and preaching"; and in still another, "fundamentalist." *Fundamentalist* (with a capital or a small *f*) describes "belief in the Bible's absolute and literal truth, historically and in prophecy" as well as "adherence to such belief." The use of *evangelical* to describe conservative Protestant beliefs seems to have occurred because *fundamentalist* developed the connotation of closed mindedness. In general, use *evangelical* unless the implication of closed mindedness is desired or a specific group or person prefers to be called a *fundamentalist*

everyone/every one *Everyone* means "every person, everybody," and refers to them as a single entity taking a singular verb <*Everyone* is busy tonight> <Hey, *everyone,* come on>. *Every one* means "each person or thing," describing them in relation to a group <*Every one* of my books will be a best seller>; this phrase also takes a singular verb

everyone . . . his/ . . . his or her/ . . . their Perhaps one of the most challenging linguistic problems brought on by the advent of nonsexist English is the question of whether to use *his, his or her,* or *their* <*Everyone* has *his* favorite TV show> <*Everyone* has *his or her* favorite TV show> <*Everyone* has *their* favorite TV show>. *His* is the grammatically and historically correct choice, but its implicit notion that *everyone* is male is offensive. *His or her* is grammatically correct but horrendously cumbersome, especially if it has to be repeated several times in a paragraph. And the popularly used *their,* which may in time be considered correct, is not thought so at this writing and offends the ears and eyes of most people who care about proper usage. Another possibility is to rewrite a sentence so a pronoun isn't needed <*Everyone* has a favorite TV show> or use a more specific plural subject instead <All Americans have *their* favorite TV shows>

evoke/invoke Some blurring has occurred between these two words, but it is still possible to tell the difference between them. *Evoke* means "to bring to mind" <Whenever I see Linda she *evokes* memories of a very happy time> or "to elicit or produce" <It's hard to *evoke* a response from such a shy person>. *Invoke* means "to call upon or for" <*invoke* the forgiveness of the Lord> or "to implement" <*invoke* the War Powers Act>. Both words are used to mean "to conjure" <*evoke* a spell> or "to cite approvingly" <Pan-Africanists *invoke* the writings of Kwame Nkrumah>, although *invoke* is preferred in these cases

exceedingly/excessively If a car were going *exceedingly* fast, it would be moving "unusually" fast. If it went *excessively* fast, it would be going "beyond a reasonable degree" of speed. *Exceedingly* is "very," but *excessively* is "too"

except/accept *see* **accept**

exceptional/exceptionable Something described as *exceptional* is "extraordinary; the exception" <an *exceptional* wine that's remarkably tasty but inexpensive>. When described as *exceptionable,* however, it's "objectionable" <an *exceptionable* wine that's remarkably bitter and overpriced> *see* **egregious/outstanding/exceptional**

excuse/pardon *see* **pardon**

exercise/exorcise To *exercise* is "to exert or use one's body" <After working on this book for months, I could use some *exercise*>. To *exorcise* (or *exorcize)* is "to rid one's soul or psyche" <*exorcise* the demons in him> <*exorcise* the desire to *exercise*>

ex officio Contrary to what logic might imply, *ex officio* does not mean "former official." It means "by virtue of office or position" <The chairing officer is *ex officio* a member of the executive committee>

exotic/esoteric *Exotic* means "very strange; unusual" or "from another country or region" <Lions are not *exotic* in Kenya>. *Esoteric* is "known or understood by a small group" or "confidential" <*esoteric* beliefs of the Moonies>

expecting/expectant/pregnant All three words can mean "carrying an embryo or fetus in the womb." *Expecting* is an informal euphemism, a shorthand way of saying "expecting the birth of a child." The more formal-sounding euphemism is *expectant,* and the more scientific-sounding term is *pregnant.* The tone of the writing should determine the choice

explode/implode *see* **implode**

extant/extent *Extant* means "existing" or "not lost" <the *extant* poetry of T. S. Eliot>, while *extent* is "the distance, degree, or limit of something" <the *extent* of his arrogance>

extemporaneous/improvised *Improvised* means "made up or created on the spot" <an *improvised* solo lasting three days>, which is also one meaning of *extemporaneous.* But *extemporaneous* is generally used to mean "without notes or text," and is said of public speakers <Donahue's *extemporaneous* diatribe>

fallacious/false *Fallacious* is used to describe things that aren't true but that are probably unintentionally untrue, as in "based on mistaken logic," "deceptive," or "misleading" <a *fallacious* argument>. *False* can also mean "based on mistaken logic," but it's generally used to describe something as "intentionally untrue" <a *false* description>, "not genuine" <*false* diamonds>, or "disloyal; unfaithful" <a *false* friend>

famed/famous Both terms mean "widely renowned" and can be used as synonyms

farther/further *Farther* is generally used when physical distances are being described <moving *farther* from New York>, while *further* is more usual when describing metaphorical distance <Union and management reps were *further* apart>. *Further* is also used to mean "additional" <No *further* work is needed>, and as a sentence modifier <*Further,* we feel extra pay should be forthcoming>, senses for which *farther* should not be employed

fatal/fateful *Fatal* is mostly used to mean "causing death" <a *fatal* car crash> or "causing destruction" <Bad reviews can be *fatal* to a movie>, but it can also mean "related to fate" <Her arrival at that moment was a *fatal* turn of events> or "decisive and affecting one's future" <It's best not to rush into a *fatal* decision like marriage>. In these last two senses it shares meanings with *fateful,* which can also mean "marked by prophecy" <a *fateful* evening during which the future became clear to us> and "decisive" <the *fateful* campaign swing>. *Fateful* can also be used to mean "deadly" or "catastrophic," but these senses are more usually conveyed by *fatal*

faze/phase *Faze* is a verb meaning "to disconcert, disrupt, or bother" <We were *fazed* by the flashing light>. *Phase,* used mostly as a noun, means "one part of a sequence" <the fourth *phase* of our plans> or "a stage of development" <the me-me-me *phase* children go through>; as a verb it can be used with *in* to mean "to introduce" <*phase* in the new cars> or with *out* to mean "to eliminate" <*phase* out those styles>

feasible/possible The main differentiation here is that *feasible* is "likely," "reasonable," or "practical to carry out" <Walking is a *feasible* activity for the ambulatory>. *Possible* is "able to be carried out given the right circumstances" <Walking is a *possible* activity for the disabled only with the proper assistance>

female/woman *Female* is a classifying term, as applicable to humans as to dogs, cats, or plants, meaning "one that bears young or produces eggs." When speaking or writing of humans, unless a good reason for classifying exists it's best to use *woman* to describe female human beings <the few *women* left in the place> <A *woman* helps>. If *female* is used, *male* (not *man)* is the acceptable counterpart <seven *female* students and one male> *see* **male/man**

fewer/less Both words mean "not as many," but they are used in different contexts. *Fewer* is generally employed when the subject is a plural number of identifiable things <*fewer* toys> <*fewer* agenda items> <*fewer* places>. *Less* is used for plural numbers when they deal with distances and amounts <*less* than a hundred dollars> <*less* than four miles> <seven pages or *less*>, as well as for singular items <*less* time than it takes to spit> <*less* material> <*less* work>. In phrases that give plural quantities of time, either word is acceptable <*less* than five minutes> <*fewer* than five minutes>, but singular amounts of time take *less* <*less* than a minute>. Despite all these rules—or perhaps because of them—many people use *less* when they should use *fewer,* and vice versa <*fewer* than four miles> <*less* toys>, and have been doing so for about a thousand years. But they are still not considered interchangeable

fiddle/violin *Fiddle* has been used to describe a small stringed instrument since the thirteenth century, while *violin* has only been in use since the sixteenth century. But the proper term in late-twentieth-century usage is *violin. Fiddle* is the name used by country-music afficionados, by others who are being informal or disparaging <What do you call the noise you're making on that *fiddle?*>, and it can also be used informally to name other related instruments <bass *fiddle*>

fill/satiate *see* satiate

finance/fund *see* fund

firm/corporation A *firm* is "a business partnership of two or more people" or "the name used by a partnership" <the *firm* of Bumblebee and Weatherby> and is generally not a legal entity in and of itself. A *corporation* is a legal entity, one that's been incorporated to conduct business <Wilner's *corporation* went broke but he still made a bundle>. The difference is made obvious by this comparison: You could sue a *corporation,* but you could only sue the members of a *firm,* not the *firm* itself

firstly/first When listing several items within a paragraph, there's a tendency to enumerate inconsistently <*First* there's money, secondly there's opportunity, and thirdly there's the personnel>. If *secondly* and *thirdly* are employed, the list should start with *firstly.* But no one starts a list with *firstly,* because it sounds funny. The solution is to enumerate the other points without an *ly* ending <*First* there's money, second there's opportunity, and third there's the personnel>

flaccid/flabby Both words mean "lacking firmness" <a *flaccid* belly> <a *flabby* belly>. They also have the additional sense "weak; feeble" <a *flabby* presidency> <a *flaccid* organization>. In any sense they are interchangeable

flagrant/blatant *see* blatant

flail/flay To *flail* is "to hit or move as if hitting with a hand-held thresher" <*flail* about in the water>. To *flay* is "to skin," "to lash," "to strip or plunder," or "to fiercely criticize." The sense "to lash" is close to the meaning of *flail* but differs in the way hitting differs from whipping

flair/flare *Flair* is "skill; talent" <a *flair* for English> or "style" <dressing with a *flair*>. A *flare* is "a glaring light" <Send up a *flare* if you're lost>, "an outburst" <a *flare* of egotistical temper>, or "a part that spreads outward" <the *flare* at the vessel's mouth>; *flare* is also used in related senses as a verb

flak/flack *Flak* means "antiaircraft artillery," "antiaircraft shells" <the *flak* bursting about the airplane>, or in a slang extension of the term, "criticism" <Don't give me *flak* about my choices>. *Flack,* an obsolete term in British English, is used in U.S. slang to mean "a publicist" or "information disseminated by a publicist" <The casting director is inundated with *flack*>

flammable/inflammable While logic might dictate that these words are opposites, the English language has never let simple logic get in its way. Thus we have *flammable,* "able to be set aflame," and *inflammable,* "able to be set aflame." *Inflammable* also has the sense "easily excited or disturbed" <an *inflammable* kind of guy>, a meaning not shared by *flammable*

flatulence/afflatus *see* **afflatus**

flaunt/flout In its undisputed sense, *flaunt* means "to display ostentatiously" <When you've got it, *flaunt* it>. It also shares the meaning of *flout* "to treat with contempt" <The judge told her it was the last time she'd

flout the law of the land>, but many careful writers consider it incorrect to use *flaunt* in this sense

flier/flyer Either spelling is acceptable, regardless of whether the sense is "one who flies," "an adventuresome gambit" <He'll take a *flier* on that Amazon trip>, or "an advertising circular" <the Woolworth's *flyer*>

flotsam/jetsam/flotsam and jetsam *Flotsam* is "floating debris," while *jetsam* is "debris that has washed ashore or sunken." Individually, or joined in the familiar *flotsam and jetsam,* they mean "vagrant people" or "miscellaneous material"

flounder/founder To *flounder* is "to move clumsily" <Steinbrenner *floundered* from one bad trade to the next> or "to seek a foothold with difficulty" <climbers *floundering* on the rocky cliff>. To *founder* is "to become disabled," "to sink" <Our little craft *foundered* in heavy seas>, or "to fail" <Her enterprise *foundered* when the funds ran out>

foam/froth Whether a substance *foams* or *froths,* a mass of bubbles forms on its surface. Either word is as good as the other to describe it

fog/haze *see* **haze**

footprints/footsteps A *footprint* is "the mark left by a foot on a surface" <How did *footprints* get on the walls?>. A *footstep* is "a step taken by a foot," "the distance a foot travels in one step" <just a *footstep* away>, "the sound of a foot stepping" <He could hear *footsteps* coming up behind him>, or "a footprint" <Purple *footsteps* began appearing all over town>. It's best to use *foot-*

print for the visible mark and *footstep* for the other senses given here

forbear/forebear To *forbear* an activity is "to refrain from" it <*forbear* opening other people's mail> or "to stop" it <*forbear* smoking>. It's important, too, to forbear the reflex to put *from* after *forbear;* it's not only unnecessary, it's incorrect to say *forbear from. Forebear,* which unfortunately has the variant spelling *forbear,* means "ancestor" <our *forebears* brought forth>. To avoid confusion, use *forebear* to mean "one who came be*fore*" and *forbear* to mean "to restrain from"

forcible/forceful/forced Although close in meaning, these words are used differently. *Forcible* is employed to mean "accomplished by physical force" <*forcible* ejection from the theater>. *Forceful* describes someone or something as "powerful in nature or character" <a *forceful* presence in the orchestra>. *Forced* is generally used to mean either "produced through great effort" <*forced* charm> or "obtained through physical force or the threat of force" <*forced* conscription>

foreword/preface While some sources are more rigid than others in differentiating these terms, *The Chicago Manual of Style,* which is the bible of book publishing, dictates that a *foreword* is an introduction to a book written by someone other than the book's author, but a *preface* is the author's own introduction to the work <There wasn't enough money to get a big-name *foreword* for this tome, so a *preface* will have to do>

fortunate/fortuitous That which is *fortunate* is "characterized by unexpected good results" <It was *fortunate* we met, or I would never have fallen in love with you>.

Fortuitous, on the other hand, is "unplanned; accidental," and can be good, bad, or in between <Our meeting so far from home is certainly *fortuitous*>

forward/foreword *Forward* can be an adjective, an adverb, a noun, or a verb, all having to do with the front; the following entry defines the adjectival and adverbial senses in detail. A *foreword* is "an introduction to a book written by someone other than the author." What's surprising is that even book authors sometimes confuse one for the other

forward/forwards *Forward* is the only correct form if the word is being used as an adjective meaning "at the front" <a *forward* cabin>, "going toward the front" <*forward* motion>, "sexually or socially aggressive" <a *forward* young man>, "advanced" <a *forward* little girl who can spell before she's three>, "progressive" <a socially conscious, *forward* kind of group>, or "future oriented" <a *forward* thinker>. The same form serves in the adverbial senses "toward the front" or "to the future" <Let's move *forward* on the issue>, which can also be expressed as *forwards* <Step *forwards* into the light>. *Forward* is generally preferred in U.S. usage

founder/flounder *see* **flounder**

Frankenstein The title of the book written by Mary Shelley is *Frankenstein,* which is the name of the mad doctor who patched together pieces of cadavers to create a monster. The monster has no proper name, but is properly called *Frankenstein's monster*

freak/freakish "Sudden and unusual in the extreme" is the most often used meaning of these interchangeable adjectives <a *freak* accident> <a *freakish* turn of events>. Some lexicographers ignore or forbid the use of *freak* as an adjective, preferring the much older *freakish,* but modern usage is overtaking these pedants

fulsome/bountiful From its sound, *fulsome* should be synonymous with *bountiful,* but it's not—at least not anymore. *Fulsome* means "offensive" or "excessive and insincere" <His flattery was *fulsome* praise indeed, each word dripping with insincerity>. Even though it originally meant "abundant," *fulsome* has come to carry the sense of "too full," which has replaced the original sense. "Abundant" is best served by *bountiful* <heaped *bountiful* praise on her> to avoid the confusion even careful writers encounter with *fulsome*

functionality This word is the noun form of the adjective *functional,* which is the adjective form of the noun *function.* Is there such a word as *functionality?* Yes. Should anyone use the word *functionality?* No. Other than being a pompously inflated way of saying something simple, it really has no *functionality*—er, function—in decent writing

fund/finance These terms are interchangeable in the verb sense "to provide capital for" <*fund* a new literacy program> <*finance* the space shuttle>. There is a tendency to use *fund* for ventures that will not produce a profit and *finance* for profit-making enterprises, but this tendency doesn't preclude using either word regardless of what the money is being spent for

fundamentalist/evangelical *see* **evangelical**

funeral director/mortician/undertaker A *funeral director* arranges and manages funerals. A *mortician* or *un-*

dertaker—the words are synonyms—is "one who prepares a body for burial and arranges and manages funerals." Most *funeral directors* are also *morticians,* and *funeral director* is a term used by *undertakers* to make an unpalatable profession seem less unpleasant

funny/amusing In senses having to do with humor, *funny* and *amusing* can be used interchangeably <That joke is not *funny*> <Some of the examples in this book are *amusing*>. But *funny* suggests stronger humor and heartier reactions, including loud laughter <Hughes is so *funny* he ought to be appearing on stage somewhere>, while *amusing* implies mild humor and pleased, but hardly riotous, reactions <Her Majesty can really be quite *amusing* when she wants to be>

further/farther *see* farther

G

gale/hurricane/typhoon *see* **typhoon**

gambit/move/opportunity *Gambit* describes a bit of chess strategy used during one's opening move and has been broadened to mean "an opening move," which makes the phrase *opening gambit* an obvious redundancy <My *gambit* at seminars is to make everyone sit up front>. A *move* is "any one of a sequence of actions" <My next *move* at seminars is to have them all take off their clothes>. *Opportunity* is not any sort of move at all, but rather "a propitious time or circumstance" <If the seminar gets past that point, there's an *opportunity* for everyone to have a lot of fun>

gamut/gauntlet Both words are used in otherwise identical phrases—*run the gamut* and *run the gauntlet*—but they have nothing else in common. The *gamut* (never *a gamut*) is "the full extent of anything" <Automotive

problems run the *gamut* from fouling spark plugs to total wrecks>. A *gauntlet* (also spelled *gantlet)* is "two lines of people who will beat someone forced to run between them" <forced the cadet to run the *gauntlet*>, "a protective glove," or "a challenge" <throw down the *gauntlet*>

garbage/trash/debris *see* **debris**

garnish/garnishee Perhaps because it's hard for the ear or eye to believe there could be such a verb as *garnishee,* these are often thought synonymous in their verb forms. They're not. *Garnish* is "to decorate food" <I'd like to *garnish* dinner with parsley>. *Garnishee* is "to take by legal process from a debtor" <I'd like to *garnishee* your salary but can't get a court order>

garret/garrote A *garret,* "a top-floor room," was once a popular place for writers to live and work. A *garrote* (also spelled *garotte)* was never popular; it's "an iron collar and screw used to execute by strangulation" or "a strangulation"

gaseous/gassy *Gaseous* is "of or existing as a gas" <hydrogen in its *gaseous* form>. *Gassy* is "containing or full of gas" <You get pretty *gassy* after eating chili>. If a person were to become *gaseous,* he or she would vanish in the ether; the correct word for intestinal distress is *gassy*

gauntlet/gantlet Both spellings are acceptable for "a protective glove," "a challenge," or "two lines of people prepared to beat someone forced to run between them"

gastronome/gourmet/epicure *see* **epicure**

gazetteer/atlas A *gazetteer* is "a geographical dictionary or index." One can often be found at the back of an *atlas,* "a bound collection of maps"

geezer/geyser "An old man, especially an odd old man," is a *geezer* <Get a load of that *geezer*>. A *geyser* is "a hot spring that spews water and steam into the air" <Old Faithful isn't the most impressive *geyser* in the world>

gel/jell Simply put, *gel* is a noun and *jell* is a verb. *Gel* is short for *gelatin,* which is "a specific kind of jelly made from the protein of animal parts" or "a thin colored sheet placed over theatrical lights," while *jell* means "to congeal; to become jelly or jellylike" <Wait for the pudding to *jell*>

gender/sex Aside from the fact that *gender* applies to grammar and *sex* generally does not, the two are interchangeable in the sense "classification as male and female" <What's its *gender?*> <I can't tell its *sex*>

genuine/authentic Both words signify "actual" or "real," but in slightly different senses. *Genuine* implies "not counterfeited or altered; verifiably what it is supposed to be" <*genuine* diamonds>. *Authentic* means "completely trustworthy; historically reliable" <period furniture made with *authentic* details>. *Genuine* antiques are things made a long time ago; *authentic* antiques may have been made more recently, but they are meticulously crafted to exactly resemble the real things

genus/genius A *genus* is "a biological, logical, or other class of grouping" <a subliterate *genus* of high

school graduates>. A *genius* is "one with superior intellectual powers" <She's not really a *genius,* just a grind who studies hard>

genus/species *Genus* is the larger category in biology, one made up of several related *species;* several *genuses* then make up a family. The *genus* name, which begins with an initial capital, is the first word in the *species* name <one *species, Homo sapiens,* that's part of the *genus Homo*>

geometric/geometrical Although *geometric* is somewhat more frequently used than *geometrical,* the two are interchangeable adjectives meaning "of or relating to geometry"

gesticulate/gesture Both words indicate "vigorous bodily movements used as a complement to speech." *Gesticulate,* a verb, has no additional meanings <He punched the air as he spoke, *gesticulating* as he described what he'd do to his former friend>. But *gesture* can also mean "bodily movements used instead of speech" <She *gestured* toward the door> or "a symbolic or courteous action or statement" <a *gesture* of my sincerity>

get/got/gotten The simple past tense of *get*—"to receive, obtain, understand," and dozens of other senses—is *got* <I *got* the ball yesterday>. *Got* and *gotten* are both past participles of *get,* meaning that they are used in the passive voice, but they function differently. When the sense is "belongs to" or "has to," the right choice is *got* <We have *got* a pleasant home> <She's *got* to go home now>. In other senses, *gotten* is the acceptable choice in American English <He'd only *gotten* as far as Bayonne when the car broke down>

ghetto/slum A *ghetto* is "a section of a city in which members of a single religious, racial, or ethnic minority live because of social or economic pressures." A *slum* is "a section of a city characterized by run-down buildings and extreme poverty." So *ghetto* refers to the people who live in a place, while *slum* describes a place itself

gibe/jibe/jib *see* **jib**

gilt/guilt *Gilt* is "a thin layer of gold or goldlike material" <the *gilt* on a picture frame>. *Guilt* is "remorse" or "responsibility for a wrong" <*guilt* over the child's injuries>

gimmick/trick In their confusable senses, both a *gimmick* and a *trick* are designed to deceive. *Gimmick* is usually "a device used to deceive," such as a mechanism that controls a gambling wheel or one employed by a magician. A *trick* is "an act of deception," whether or not a *gimmick* is involved in that deception

glance/glimpse Both a *glance* and a *glimpse* are "a brief look," but while *glance* is "to take a quick look," *glimpse* is "to have a quick look" <*Glance* out the window and you may *glimpse* an amazing sight>. *Glimpse* also is sometimes used to suggest incomplete viewing <a *glimpse* of his naked form, sufficient only to tantalize>

good/well Informal or idiomatic writing and speech aside, in proper usage *good* is the adjective <I smell *good*> and *well* is the adverb <I smell *well*>. *Well* can also function as an adjective meaning "healthy" or "proper," but in senses having to do with positive qualities in general, *good* modifies the subject of a sentence and *well* modifies the activity occurring in that sentence

gourmet/gourmand A *gourmet* is "one who is knowledgeable of and enjoys fine food and wine." "One who enjoys eating well" without the kind of knowledge enjoyed by a gourmet is called a *gourmand* (also spelled *gormand)* <The *gourmet* at the table explained why the *gourmands* would enjoy this repast> *see* **epicure/gastronome/gourmet**

gratified/grateful *Gratified* is "pleased or satisfied" <He was *gratified* by their accomplishment> or "humored or indulged" <She *gratified* her peculiar tastes>. *Grateful* carries one sense of *gratified* in a different form with the meaning "satisfying or pleasing" <a night of *grateful* diversions>, but this sense is not used very commonly. In its more usual meanings, *grateful* can be "thankful" <*grateful* for your handouts> or "expressing thankfulness" <The least you could do is be *grateful*>

gratuitous A term with two meanings, gratuitous can be either "free; unearned" <gave them a *gratuitous* bottle of cheer> or "unwarranted; undeserved" <a *gratuitous* insult>

graze/browse *see* **browse**

grey/gray "A shade or color between black and white" is called *grey* in British English and *gray* in U.S. English

griddle/skillet A *griddle* is "a flat pan or other flat metal cooking surface," one without sides, but a *skillet* is "a shallow pan," one with short sides <Pancakes are cooked on a *griddle,* but sauces are easier to contain if cooked in a *skillet*>

grip/grippe The first term describes "a firm grasp," the second, "influenza" <The whole family was in the *grip* of *grippe*>. *Grippe* is often used with *the.* Lest it seem too easy, some dictionaries give *grip* as a variant spelling of *grippe,* but it's best to use *grippe* for the illness

ground/terrain *see* **terrain**

grueling/gruesome Although they sound similar, something *grueling* is "arduous, exhausting" <a *grueling* day at the office>, but something *gruesome* is "horrible, revolting" <a *gruesome* accident>

guarantee/guaranty Dictionary entries for these words might lead one to believe there is some basic difference between them, but careful scrutiny reveals that either can be used to mean "an assurance," "a promise or pledge," "something held as security," or "one who promises, assures, or secures something." *Guarantee* is the more common spelling of the verb form

guerrilla/gorilla A *guerrilla* (often spelled *guerilla)* is "a combatant in unconventional warfare" <the so-called contra *guerrillas*>. The large hairy ape that seems so human is called a *gorilla*

guilt/gilt *see* **gilt**

gulf/bay/sound *see* **bay**

habitat/environment Whether talking about people, plants, or animals, a *habitat* is "the place or type of place in which someone or something lives"; when applied to people, "a home" <Most middle-class folks prefer a *habitat* with at least a quarter-acre of land>. The *environment* is "the combination of factors that influence or affect someone or something's life" <If you decide on a college *environment* you'll find it revolves around ideas and office politics>. A home is never correctly referred to as an *environment*

hail/hale Meanings of *hail* include "precipitation in the form of frozen balls" and "a greeting or act of calling" as well as "to greet or call for" <*hail* a taxi>. That form is also used in the expression *hail-fellow-well-met.* The other *hale* means "healthy; sound" <*hale* and hearty> or, in less-used senses, "pull" and "force to go"

hair/hare/heir *Hair* grows on top of your head. A *hare* is a rabbit. And an *heir* (pronounced like *air)* is "one who inherits from a predecessor"

half-mast/half-staff Either term is acceptable for the intended meaning "a position approximately halfway down a flagpole"

hanged/hung Both words are past tense forms of the verb *hang,* and both can be accepted in most senses. *Hanged* is more usual when the meaning is "suspended by the neck until dead," especially for officially sanctioned executions <She was *hanged* at sunrise>. Most other senses are better served by *hung* <*hung* his head and cried> <*hung* up the phone> <the curveball *hung*>

happen/transpire *see* **transpire**

harbor/port Both a *harbor* and a *port* can be "a haven or refuge" and "a sheltered part of a body of water deep enough for ships to cast anchor in," but a *port* has the added sense of "a town with shipping facilities located at a body of water" <My least favorite *port* is Elizabeth, New Jersey>

hard-boiled/hard-cooked Although some usage experts appear to want to make a mountain out of a molehill about these terms, there's not even much of a molehill here. Almost everyone uses *hard-boiled* to describe well-cooked eggs, which is also what's listed in most dictionaries; if you prefer *hard-cooked,* go ahead and use it

hardly ever/almost never *Hardly ever* and *almost never* both mean "very rarely" and can be used interchangeably <We *hardly ever* see Diane and George anymore> <They *almost never* see us either>

hardy/hearty Although they sound alike and have some meanings that are similar, these words are not synonymous in any senses. *Hardy* means "strong" <a *hardy* draft animal>, "courageous" <*hardy* soldiers preparing for the offensive>, "brazen" <a daring daylight robbery perpetrated by *hardy* criminals>, "able to withstand cold weather" <You have to be pretty *hardy* to swim in the ocean in January>, or "able to survive the winter outdoors" <*hardy* perennials>. *Hearty* is "warmly cordial" <a *hearty* greeting>, "vigorously healthy" <*hearty* young women able to work long days>, "unequivocal" <*hearty* support>, or "filling and nourishing" <a *hearty* meal>

have/of *see* of

haze/fog *Fog* can cause *haze,* but *haze* is not necessarily *fog. Haze* is "moisture, smoke, dust, or vapor suspended in the air close to the ground and obscuring visibility" <Demolition in the apartment below us filled our home with a *haze* of plaster dust>. *Fog* is "cloudlike water vapor suspended in the air close to the ground and obscuring visibility" <The *fog* rolled in at sunset>. Either *haze* or *fog* can be used to describe a muddled mental state <She's in a *haze* this morning> <an alcoholic *fog*>

he/him Strict adherence to the rules of grammar requires use of *he* when the verb "to be" is employed <I wanted the winner to be *he*>. No matter how grammatically valid, however, no one uses this formulation in spoken English, and very few would write it in even the most formal contexts. Unless grammatic perfection is required, it's best to judge such sentences by the way they sound. If perfection is required, write the sentence differently <I wanted *him* to win>

healthy/healthful *Healthy* describes the condition of humans and other animals; it means "disease-free, vigorous, and well" <a *healthy* Olympic team>. *Healthful* can have the same meaning, essentially "full of health," but it is generally used to mean "contributing to health" in reference to things that are good for you <*healthful* food and drink>

heaved/hove Both words form the past tense of the verb *heave,* "to toss, throw, or lift," although *hove* is more common in nautical use <he *hove* that line> <*heaved* a sigh of relief>

hesitation/hesitancy Both terms are noun forms of *hesitate* and mean "an act of hesitating" or "indecision" <My *hesitation* may cause some *hesitancy* on your part>. *Hesitation* also has the sense "a faltering of speech" <Harold's *hesitation* when trying to explain things to Erin turned into full-scale stuttering>

his/his or her/their *see* everyone . . . his

historic/historical *Historic* and *historical* are both used to mean "important or famous in history," but their senses diverge to some extent. *Historic* applies to those people or events that will or have become history <a *historic* ball game> <this *historic* presidency>. *Historical* refers to those things that are about history <*historical* novels> <a play with *historical* themes>

hole/whole That which is an absence or void where something formerly was is a *hole* <a *hole* in my shoe>.

That which has no hole in it, or is otherwise complete and intact, is *whole* <loves me with her *whole* being>

Holland/the Netherlands *Holland* is the informal name applied to the country that is formally *the Netherlands.* North Holland and South Holland are two counties in the modern kingdom of *the Netherlands.* To be correct, use *the Netherlands;* to be understood, either term will do

home/house/dwelling *see* **dwelling**

homonym/synonym *Homonyms* are two or more words that sound the same and are often spelled the same but have different meanings <*Be* and *bee* are *homonyms*>. *Synonyms* are words with the same meanings <*Healthful* and *healthy* are *synonyms* in the sense "full of health">

hopeful/optimistic *Hope* has to do with the desire for a good outcome, while *optimism* is the belief in such an outcome. To be *hopeful* is to be "tending toward hope" <I'm *hopeful* we can finish the job next week> or "inspiring of hope" <She's such a *hopeful* influence on the chronic-care ward>. *Optimistic* is "tending toward the most positive outlook possible" <remained *optimistic* about the Yankees' chances despite a twelve-game losing streak>

hopefully One of the words that give authorities on grammar and usage such fits is *hopefully.* Its undisputed meaning is "in a manner inclined toward hope" <He listened *hopefully* to her every word, waiting for her to declare her love>. It is when it's used to modify a whole sentence with the meaning "it is hoped" that *hopefully* arouses a lot of hostility <*Hopefully,* we'll all still be around in the twenty-first century>. When dissected in a technically correct fashion, this example would read "We'll still be here in the year 2000 and will still be full of hope," which of course is not what's meant. Another objection to this usage is that it's become an overused cliché, and to some extent this is true. But to say "It is hoped we'll all still be here" is stiff and pedantic, which isn't good usage either. *Hopefully* is no doubt here to stay in the sense "it is hoped," regardless of what the keepers of the flame have to say about it. But let the speaker and, to a greater extent, the writer beware that such usage will raise howls of disapproval in many quarters

horrible/horrid In some dictionaries the definitions of these two terms are the same, but there is still a shade of difference in the ways they're used. *Horrible* tends to be the stronger word, meaning "causing or marked by horror" <*horrible* devastation resulting from an earthquake>. *Horrid* is "offensive, loathsome" <the *horrid* smell of year-old milk>, but usually not quite so full of horror as *horrible*

house/home/dwelling *see* **dwelling**

hove/heaved *see* **heaved**

however/how ever *However* is used as an adverb to mean "by whatever means" <*however* it gets done> or "to whatever extent," and as a conjunction in the senses "but" or "yet" <She'll do it. *However,* I'm not sure she's the best candidate>. The two-word form is used for emphasis only in questions with the meaning "by whatever means" <*How ever* did he get it done?>

hue/color/tint All three of these terms help define objects in relation to the way light is reflected or absorbed by them. The basic word is *color,* which describes something's main reflective appearance <the *color* red> <What *color* are the team's uniforms?>. *Hue* is, in technical terms, "one aspect of color that has to do with a scale of perception" as well as "a particular gradation of color" or "a pale coloration" <a yellowish *hue* over the whole city>. In this last sense, *hue* is synonymous with *tint,* although *tint* also refers to "any lighter or darker shades of a given color" <green with a heavy *tint* of orange>

hue/hew As described in the previous entry, *hue* is "a pale coloration" or "a particular gradation of color." *Hew* is "to cut or fashion with an ax, knife, or other tool" <She can *hew* a canoe from a fallen birch>

human/human being/person *Human* and *human being* stem from scientific usage, meaning "a member of the genus *Homo* and the species *Homo sapiens,*" but their use has since expanded into nonscientific areas as well. They are still used primarily to denote those aspects that distinguish us from other animals <War is something *humans* seem unable to avoid> <A *human being* would have cried in those circumstances>. *Person* stems from an ancient Latin word for actor and still carries "a character in a play" as one of its meanings. But in more general use it refers to "an individual," "a self" <A *person* could develop the grippe>, or "an entity entitled to recognition under the law" <A *person* has the right to live in peace>

humorous/comical *see* **comical**

hung/hanged *see* **hanged**

hurricane/gale/typhoon *see* **typhoon**

hypoallergenic/nonallergenic/allergic/allergenic *see* **allergic**

hypothetical/possible Something that's *hypothetical* is "based on an assertion, premise, or supposition" <*hypothetical* equality between the sexes>, "uncertain" <prospects for victory being *hypothetical* at best>, or "contingent" <a *hypothetical* result based on her participation>. Something that's *possible* is "achievable under the circumstances" <one *possible* outcome of this meeting>, which does not necessitate an assertion or premise as the starting point, something that *hypothetical* usually requires

I/me In most contexts there is no problem choosing between *me* and *I; I* appears before the verb <*I* don't like you> and *me* appears after the verb <You'd better pick *me*>. But confusion arises when self-reference is needed for the second of a pair of pronouns <between you and *me* (or *I*)>, for placement immediately following any form of the verb *be* <It is *I* (or *me*)>, or for a comparison using *than* or *as* <better than *me* (or *I*)>. In all these cases, *me* has become accepted, if not preferred, especially in speech <between you and *me*> <It's *me*> <better than *me*>. Formal usage, however, especially in writing, demands the use of *I* after *be* <It is *I*> and after *than* when the first part of the comparison is the subject of the verb <She looks better than *I*>; *me* is correct in formal usage as the second of a pair of pronouns <between you and *me*>

ibid./op. cit. *Ibid.,* short for *ibidem,* "in the same place," is used with a page number in footnotes to refer to the immediately preceding footnote <1. Paul Heacock, *Which Word When?* (New York: Dell Publishing Co., 1989), p. 96. 2. *Ibid.,* p. 135>. *Op. cit.,* short for *opere citato,* "in the work cited," is used with an author's name and a page number as a shorthand reference subsequent to the first citation <27. Heacock, *op. cit.,* p. 156>. Because of the confusion that can occur if, for instance, two books by Heacock were cited earlier, or if the first reference to Heacock's book was deleted from the finished piece, many style guides recommend against using *op. cit.* at all

-ible/-able *see* **-able**

identical to/identical with Neither choice is more correct than the other in this case

ideologue/demagogue A *demagogue* could be an *ideologue,* but the two don't necessarily mean the same thing. An *ideologue* is "an adherent to an ideology," "an advocate," or "an impractical theorist" <Marx could certainly be considered an *ideologue*>. A *demagogue* is "one who leads by appealing to emotions" <Reagan was a *demagogue,* especially compared with Carter>

idiot/moron *see* **moron**

idle/idyll *Idle* is an adjective meaning "inactive," "unemployed," or "useless" <*idle* gossip>. *Idyll* is a noun meaning "a descriptive work of literature about a peaceful, contented rural life" or "an event appropriate for such a work" <Our weekend at the country house provided us with such a relaxing *idyll*>

i.e./e.g. *see* **e.g.**

if/that In most of their functions *if* and *that* are not at all confusable <I'll go home *if* it rains> <He hopes *that* is okay>. There is, however, a point at which they become individually and jointly muddled. *If* can mean "whether" <She didn't know *if* it would rain>, which comes pretty close to the sense of *that* "used to introduce a clause giving a fact, wish, consequence, or reason" <She didn't know *that* it would rain>. In both these examples the meaning would be clearer if the sentences were rewritten. In the first example, the meaning could be "whether or not it will rain" or it could be "in the event it rains"; in the second, it could again mean "whether or not it will rain" or it could mean "she was unaware of impending rain." While some grammarians insist that *if* should never be used to mean "whether," the rule to bear in mind is that ambiguity should always be avoided. If a sentence employing *if* or *that* could be misread, rewrite it *see* **whether/if**

illegible/unreadable A simple distinction separates these terms. *Illegible* writing can't be read because the characters and words are badly formed and "undecipherable" <You'll get F's in your handwriting course if you hand in *illegible* work like that>. *Unreadable* writing can't be read because it is "uninteresting, incomprehensible, or not worth reading" <Many usage dictionaries are *unreadable*>. *Unreadable* can also be used to mean "illegible," but it's best to use *illegible* for that sense and *unreadable* in its other senses

illicit/illegal Both *illicit* and *illegal* acts are prohibited. An *illicit* act is one "prohibited by law or custom"

<An *illicit* sexual liaison may not land him in jail, but it will get him frowns on Main Street>, while an *illegal* one is "prohibited by law" <It's *illegal* to yell "fire" in a theater>

illiterate/ignorant The basic sense of *illiterate* is "unable to read or write" <Many school systems produce *illiterate* high school graduates>. This meaning has been extended to "unknowledgeable in a given field or subject" <computer *illiterate*>, and it is this sense that brushes close to the meaning of *ignorant* "generally uninformed or uneducated" or "unaware or unknowledgeable of a specific field or subject" <*ignorant* of the rules of football>

illusion/allusion An *illusion* is "a deceptive, false, or erroneous perception" <Paint the walls white if you want the *illusion* of more space>. An *allusion* is "an indirect reference, especially one with a pointed meaning" <Her *allusion* to her immediate predecessor made it plain she did not want to be disposed of in similar fashion>. Although they are completely dissimilar in meaning, they are frequently confused because they sound almost the same *see* **delusion/illusion**

illusive/elusive *see* **elusive**

illustrative/illustrious An *illustrative* thing would be one that is "clarifying, illustrating" <His *illustrative* remarks helped make sense of the rules>. An *illustrious* person or thing would be one that is "superlative, famous, eminent" <Her *illustrious* presence turned an ordinary dinner into an evening to remember>

imaginary/imaginative Although quite close in meaning, there is a difference between these words.

Imaginary is "existing only in the imagination; unreal" <an *imaginary* friend>. *Imaginative* is "characterized by use of the imagination; created by using the imagination" <an *imaginative* story>. Something *imaginative* exists in the real world; something *imaginary* doesn't

imbue/infuse *see* **infuse**

immigrate/emigrate *see* **emigrate**

imminent/eminent *see* **eminent**

immoral/amoral *see* **amoral**

immovable/irremovable *Immovable* (also spelled *immoveable*) means "physically incapable of being moved" <Without earth-movers or explosives, mountains are pretty much *immovable*>. *Irremovable* is "not removable; incapable of being taken away or dismissed" <Presidents tend to think themselves *irremovable* right up to the start of impeachment proceedings>

immunity/impunity These two words not only have similar sounds, they carry very similar meanings. *Immunity* is "exemption, freedom from, or being excused from" <testify with *immunity* from prosecution> <have an *immunity* from the flu>. *Impunity* is similarly "exemption or freedom from prosecution, harm, or loss" <She can speak with *impunity*> <Payoffs can give lawbreakers *impunity*>. The main difference is that *immunity* is applied to disease as well as social and legal activities, but *impunity* applies only to potential punishment

implicit/implied In one use these are synonyms. *Implicit* can mean "unclearly or not overtly stated or understood" <When he told me it was time to leave, the

implicit suggestion was that I'd had enough to drink>, which is identical to the meaning of *implied.* Other senses covered by *implicit* are "inherent" <Anger was *implicit* in the way he walked> and "without doubt; unequivocal" <*implicit* faith in her abilities>

implode/explode To *implode* is "to collapse inward in a violent fashion" <Picture tubes in TV sets *implode* when broken because they contain a near-vacuum>. This is the opposite of *explode,* "to collapse outward in a violent fashion" <You'd better hope the volcano doesn't *explode* while you're hiking on it>. Remember that *implode* is to collapse *i*nward

imply/infer This is one of the most hotly debated pairs of confusable words in the English language. They indisputably share the meaning "to involve as a necessary consequence" <An outcome *implies* an action> <An outcome *infers* an action>. But *imply* means "to suggest without overtly stating" <His starched shirt and tie *imply* that this is a serious meeting>, while *infer* is generally held to mean "understood by deduction" <I could *infer* the seriousness of the meeting from the way he dressed>. But to keep the waters clouded, experts as diverse as Merriam-Webster, the dictionary makers, and William Shakespeare, the writer, have held that *infer* can mean "indicate," "suggest," or "hint." These meanings of *infer* fall somewhere between the first sense given above, for which everyone agrees *imply* and *infer* are synonyms, and the senses that many experts feel belong only to *imply.* Use of *infer* in senses where *imply* would not be disputed— "indicate," "suggest," "hint"—is best avoided, unless you're prepared to carry a Merriam-Webster dictionary around with you
see **insinuate/imply**

improvised/extemporaneous *see* **extemporaneous**

impugn/imply *Impugn* means "to attack; to argue against" <She *impugned* his virtue>. *Imply,* as should be clear from the preceding entry, means "to state indirectly" <She *implied* that he was less than virtuous> *see* **malign/impugn, oppugn/impugn**

in/into *see* **into**

in/on Although generally quite distinct in meaning and usage <Get *in* the boat> <Sit *on* the seat>, there is a circumstance where confusion reigns. *In behalf of* is "acting in the best interests of" <*In behalf of* dear old Granny's health, I kept her away from the cookie jar>. *On behalf of* means "representing or acting in place of" <*On behalf of* Granny, I accept this award>

in/within *see* **within**

inalienable/unalienable If English were a simple language, there would be no need for a book such as this. It isn't, so there is. The prefixes *in-* and *un-* both mean "not" and appeared in Middle English. *In-* comes from Latin by way of Middle French, while *un-,* apparently from the same Latin root, stems from Old English. The choice between them is largely a matter of history and convention. In some instances, such as <*inalienable* rights>, the choice of one over the other is a matter of personal preference. Both words mean "not capable of being transferred or removed"

inapt/inept *Inapt* means "unlikely, unsuitable, inappropriate." *Inept* means "foolishly incompetent, lacking in skill." Alas, *inapt* is often used to mean "lacking in skill" and *inept* is often used to mean "inappropriate."

For the sake of clarity and logic, use *inapt* to mean *"inappropriate"* <His *inapt* nose-picking ruffled quite a few feathers among the guests> and *inept* for "foolishly incompetent" <an *inept* performance of *The Afro-Eurasian Eclipse*>

inartistic/unartistic *see* **unartistic**

incite/insight *see* **insight**

include/comprise These terms are synonymous in that they both mean "to contain as part of a whole" <This family *comprises* the three of us> <This family *includes* the three of us>. But *comprise* is generally used when the object of the sentence is all the elements that make up the whole subject <This family *comprises* the three of us>, while *include* is used for any of the elements individually <This family *includes* me> as well as for all of them *see* **comprise/compose**

incontinent/incompetent *Incontinent* means "unrestrained" or "unable to control urination" <paper diapers for *incontinent* adults>, the second sense being the more common. *Incompetent* is "not qualified, unsuitable, incapable, or dysfunctional" <The *incompetent* plumber fixed the boiler but forgot to turn the water back on>

inculcate/indoctrinate Although both words have to do with regimented learning, the difference between them is clear. *Inculcate* is "to teach by forceful repetition," an educational method employed in many schools <*inculcate* geometry theorems in a special all-night session>. *Indoctrinate* is "to teach uncritical acceptance of a doctrine," in effect, "to brainwash" <Right-wingers try

to *indoctrinate* the public with the notion that unrestrained capitalism solves everything>

indexes/indices Most dictionaries simply give "indexes or indices" as the plural of *index.* But *indexes* is generally preferred when the meaning is "two or more lists of words and phrases that appear in a book" <*indexes* of place names, personal names, and historical topics>, while *indices* is the proper form for "two numbers or mathematical expressions used to indicate position of an element" <*Indices* A and D position the point here>

indiscriminate/undiscriminating Some hair-splitters suggest the only proper applications of the *in-* and *un-* prefixes to *discriminate* are *indiscriminate* and *undiscriminating,* both meaning "marked by careless distinction or no distinction at all" <*indiscriminate* use of power> <*undiscriminating* use of power>, while others maintain the acceptability of *indiscriminating* in the same sense. The only genuine distinction that can be made between these terms is that *undiscriminating* means "lacking in good taste and judgment," which *indiscriminate* does not. Even a careful writer can be undiscriminating about which to use otherwise

inedible/uneatable *see* **uneatable**

inflammable/flammable *see* **flammable**

inflict/afflict Both words mean "to impose or force upon someone, especially in a painful fashion," and the only substantial difference is that *afflict* is usually used with *with* <Our grandfather was *afflicted* with a crippling disease> <*inflict* pain on others>

infuse/imbue *Infuse* and *imbue* both mean "to permeate," but *infuse* is used when aspirations, ideas, or principles are involved <*infuse* with a sense of duty>, or when tea is being made <the hot water was *infused* with the smell and taste of cinnamon>. *Imbue* is used when colors are being added <The blue cloth is then *imbued* with red, resulting in a deep purple material> or, in a metaphorical sense, when a text or other work is permeated with something <His work today is still *imbued* with the propelling bass sounds used by Mingus>; *infuse* can be used synonymously in this last sense

ingenious/ingenuous These terms not only cause confusion between them, but *ingenuous* alone leaves many readers and writers baffled. *Ingenious* is "brilliant, clever" <The inventor of the bicycle had an *ingenious* idea>. *Ingenuous* is "naive, simple" <His *ingenuous* reply made her realize he really did have no experience outside the classroom>

in line/on line There should be no confusion about these two, since either can be used. Some sticklers like to think *on* can only mean "in contact with the surface of," as in "don't stand *on* the table," but it can be used in many other senses as well. Depending on where they grew up, some Americans stand *in line* while others stand *on line*

innocent/not guilty In general use, *innocent* and *not guilty* can often be used interchangeably <He claimed to be *innocent* when asked if he pinched her> <His girlfriend believed he was *not guilty* of pinching her>. There is a shade of difference between them that's made explicit in their applications in law: *Innocent* is "wholly lawful, blameless," even "guileless, ingenuous," while *not guilty* is "not responsible or chargeable" or "not punishable" <Just because he was found *not*

guilty by a jury doesn't mean he was *innocent* of any involvement in the whole sordid mess>. Defendants in legal proceedings plead *not guilty;* their guilt is a matter for the courts to decide, while their innocence is more properly judged by a higher power

innumerable Quite literally, *innumerable* means "uncountable; too many to be numbered" <The universe is made up of *innumerable* atoms>. It does not mean, and cannot rightly be used to mean, "a lot," "a whole bunch," or "more than I have counted"

inquire/enquire *see* **enquire**

in regard to/with regard to/as regards All three of these forms are technically correct. That is, *in* and *with* are followed by the singular *regard,* and *as* is followed by the plural *regards* <*In regard to* the above-mentioned event, she was nowhere to be found at the time> <*With regard to* the time, it's almost four o'clock> <*As regards* your question, no, I do not think we should get married>. But none of the three provides a gracious turn of phrase; on the contrary, they're kind of ugly. Better to rephrase a sentence using *regarding, about, in,* or some other word or phrase <*At the time of* the above-mentioned event, she was nowhere to be found> <*Regarding* the time, it's almost four o'clock> <*As for* your question, no, I don't think we should get married>

insidious/invidious *see* **invidious**

insight/incite *Insight* is a noun meaning "intuitive understanding; a revealing knowledge"—in effect, "sight into" <After years of studying artists he had terrific *insight* into how someone's technique was reflected

in the finished work>. *Incite,* a verb, means "to inflame to action" and is often used to describe what a speaker does to a crowd that then riots <Establishment types expressed concern that Abbie would *incite* any gathering to which he lectured>

insightful/perceptive Both words have to do with understanding what's being seen, but *insightful* is "characterized by intuitive understanding" and explains the ability to understand the inner nature of something <Her *insightful* remarks made it clear she'd not only read everything there was to read on the subject but had done some thinking too>. *Perceptive* is "characterized by the ability to clearly see and understand" and deals with the external aspects of something <Her *perceptive* remarks made it clear she'd been paying close attention during the lecture>

insinuate/imply To *insinuate* means "to work in subtly and sneakily," with the emphasis on sneakily <Without their realizing it, he had been *insinuating* that they were ignorant>. To *imply* is "to state indirectly" with no connotation of worminess <His actions *implied* a real love of people>

instinct/intuition *see* **intuition**

insure/ensure/assure *see* **ensure**

integrate/desegregate Usually used when speaking about improving race relations in the U.S. and meaning "to bring together equally," they differ in emphasis. *Integrate* stresses the blending together of people with different backgrounds <try to *integrate* Vietnamese refugees into mainstream America>, while *desegregate* is more negative, since it deals just with with stopping segregation <Some might argue that while busing can *desegregate* a school system it won't harmoniously *integrate* a community>

intense/intensive *Intensive* is not simply a longer, fancier word for *intense.* Something described as *intense* is "marked by an extreme degree," which can be said of many sorts of activities <*intense* preparation before an examination> <Mattingly's *intense* concentration on the ball>. *Intensive* means "highly concentrated" and is applied to farming <*Intensive* agriculture is the application of more resources to the same amount of land>, medicine <*intensive*-care wards providing comprehensive medical care>, warfare <*Intensive* bombing raids concentrate a lot of firepower on a single target>, linguistics, and a few other technical fields. In short, *intense* is for senses where *great* would be right, while *intensive* is just for *highly concentrated*

intensive porpoises/intents and purposes Figures of speech take strange twists and turns in the minds of those who use them. This one was sighted in a college English paper. *Intensive porpoises* might be a highly concentrated group of aquatic mammals. The right form is *intents and purposes,* which means "reasons" and is used in the phrase *for all intents and purposes* to mean "for the most part" or "by and large; in essence" <The manuscript was, for all *intents and purposes,* finished before we started polishing it up>

inter/intern When people are *interred* they are put in a coffin and placed in a grave, since *inter* means "to bury" <I will *inter* my pooch on a hill overlooking her favorite fireplug>. When someone *interns,* on the other hand, it means "to gain practical experience after acquiring advanced training, as in medicine or education" <Those who *intern* at Beth Israel are often as skilled as the two-hundred-dollar-an-hour specialists>

interior/internal Basically they both mean "inside," but with slight differences in application. *Interior* usually applies to physical structures <The real estate agent suggested we ignore the way it looked when we drove up and concentrate instead on how the *interior* space could be enjoyed> or land <secretary of the *interior*>. *Internal* most often deals with the human body <An *internal* exam revealed no dilation of the cervix> or organizational relations <The *internal* struggle between the executive committee and the president had no impact on sales>

into/in *Into* describes "moving toward; entering" <We got *into* our seats>. *In* describes "existing within the confines of" <The seats were *in* our car>. *In* should be used for current location, *into* to characterize the act of entering something <While *in* our car we got *into* a traffic jam>

intra-/inter-/intro- Three prefixes that look like they could all be synonymous, yet each of these is quite different from the others. *Intra-* is combined with nouns naming places, organizations, or even body parts for "within, inside of, between layers of" <New York's own *intra*city rail service, the subway system, has deteriorated steadily for decades> <The Giants held an *intra*squad workout on off days> <*intra*muscular injections>. *Inter-* combines with all sorts of nouns and means "between" <*inter*city travel> <*inter*racial marriage><*inter*personal skills>. *Intro-* means "into, in, within" and is mostly used to describe personal activities

<*intro*mission of the penis during intercourse> or personality <*intro*verted type of guy who won't talk to anyone>. Note that all three prefixes are generally closed up, or combined without a hyphen

intuition/instinct Neither *intuition* nor *instinct* can be learned, but they are very different in meaning. The first deals with knowledge and understanding, the second with actions and abilities. *Intuition* is "knowledge without an apparent source" or "the power to know without thinking" <My *intuition* suggests that peace will soon be at hand>. *Instinct* is "inherent ability" or "natural tendency" <Her *instinct* is to go for the jugular>

invidious/insidious Something *invidious* is "promoting animosity, unrest, or resentment" <Her *invidious* remarks about the dirty habits of "those people" triggered a nasty reaction from the audience>. Something *insidious* is "sneakily attractive" or "slowly affecting" <the *insidious* impact of asbestos>

invoke/evoke *see* **evoke**

iota/scintilla *see* **scintilla**

ironic/ironical *Ironical* is simply an alternate form of *ironic,* "marked by irony" <It was *ironic* that he died of thirst just ten yards from water> <The play had an *ironical* ending>. Since the *-al* ending adds nothing but length, it's generally best to use *ironic*

irregardless/regardless There's no such word as *irregardless,* or more correctly, such a word would mean "not regardless" or "regardful." The meaning "without regard" can only be conveyed by *regardless* <I'm going

to finish this manuscript *regardless* of my health>. The popularity of *irregardless* may derive from the real word *irrespective*

irremovable/immovable *see* **immovable**

is/are Anyone who writes or speaks English has learned that *is* is singular <he, she, or it *is*>, while *are* is plural <we *are*>. Sometimes, however, the number of the subject is elusive. Is the correct form "Two times three *is* six" or "Two times three *are* six"? Is it <A couple *is* happy" or "A couple *are* happy"? In the multiplication example, the subject of the sentence is *three,* but this only confuses things further: Is it the number *three* (singular) or is it *three things* (plural)? The answer here is that either way of looking at it is okay, with the choice left to the author. The same quandary comes up in a different mathematical calculation, addition <Two plus three *is* five> <Two plus three *are* five>, but here the answer is the same. The subject can be considered to be "the sum of," which is singular, or it can be "two things plus three things," which is plural. Again, the choice is the writer's. In the example about the couple, the correct choice is *is,* since the subject (a couple) is singular, even though two individuals make up that couple *see* **either . . . is/ . . . are**

its/it's Apostrophe confusion is particularly widespread. Columnist Dave Barry has suggested that an apostrophe is used to warn readers that an *s* will follow, and although this rule is regularly employed, it's not correct. The possessive form is *its* <That is *its* dish> <Here are *its* possible outcomes>; like the possessive pronouns *his, hers,* and *theirs,* no apostrophe is used. For a contraction of *it is,* the apostrophe is employed, just as it is employed for any other contraction <*It's* a difficult job> <Why *it's* so difficult is hard to imagine>

jell/gel *see* **gel**

jetsam/flotsam/flotsam and jetsam *see* **flotsam**

jetty/pier/wharf/dock *see* **dock**

jib/jibe/gibe In their most frequently used senses, "a small triangular sail at the front of a ship" is a *jib,* "to move a ship's course or a ship's sail suddenly and forcibly from one side to the other" is to *jibe,* and "to tease" is to *gibe.* But these words are not as simple as that. *Jib* can also mean "to shift quickly from one side to the other" as well as "to refuse to move" and "the arm of a crane or boom of a derrick." And *jibe* can be a variant spelling of *gibe,* "to tease," and also means "to agree." There simply is no easy way to keep these terms straight

jibe/jive In the senses in which they're confused, *jibe* means "to agree" <That doesn't *jibe* with my recollection

of the meeting>, while *jibe* (sometimes spelled *gibe)* or *jive* can be used to mean "to tease, kid, cajole" <You keep *jiving* me about my ratty-looking beard>

judicial/judicious Although closely related in one sense, these terms cannot be interchanged. *Judicial* is used mostly to refer to "that having to do with judges, justice, or the administration of justice" <Concern was raised about Judge Bork's potential for *judicial* activism> <*Judicial* restraint can put criminals out on the streets>. In another sense, it means "judgmental, critical" <She cast a *judicial* eye on the so-called work of art>. This last sense is the closest in meaning to *judicious,* which is "characterized by sound judgment" <Cuomo thought it would not be *judicious* to run for president in 1988> <a *judicious* choice of food for a post-Thanksgiving snack>

karat/caret/carrot/carat *see* carat

kid/child Strictly speaking, a *kid* is "a young goat, antelope, or other such animal" or "the skin of these animals when used as leather" <*kid* gloves>. A *child* is "a young human being" <Never do an act with a *child* or an animal>. In formal texts this distinction should be maintained. But informal use of *kid* to mean "a child" is documented for almost four hundred years, making it understandable and permissible in many kinds of writing and most speech <*Kids* are easy to get along with if you relax and show real interest in them>

kill/stream/creek/brook/river In the aquatic sense, *kill* is "a stream, creek, or channel" and appears in the names of freshwater and saltwater bodies in the U.S. where the Dutch first settled <the Bush *Kill*> <Peeks*kill*> <the *Kill* van Kull>; because of its meaning, *kill* cannot be used with *river, channel,* and so forth when naming bodies of water <the *Kill* van Kull, not the *Kill* van Kull Channel>. A *stream* is "any body of moving water, such as a river, creek, or brook," and is mostly used generically, not in proper names <Let's sit down by that pretty little *stream* and relax awhile>. A *creek* is "a small stream of water," and often is used to name tributaries of rivers <Bowman's *Creek*> as well as generically <Marjorie soaked her feet in the *creek*>. *Brook* has the same meaning as *creek* and can be used for named and unnamed small streams. And *river* is "a large stream of water"; it, too, is used both properly <Hudson *River*> and generically <down by the river>. One final differentiation needs to be pointed out: When you go *up the river* you are being sent to jail; when you're *up a creek* you're in a very difficult situation

kind/kindly Although words ending in *ly* are generally adverbs, it's not always the case. Both these words mean "friendly, warmhearted, agreeable, pleasant" when used as adjectives, and either can be used to describe people and their natures <He's a *kind* old soul> <She's got a *kindly* disposition>. When describing considerate or sympathetic acts, however, *kindly* is more commonly used <That thousand-dollar check was a *kindly* gift indeed> <a *kindly* expression of concern for the deceased's family>

kind of/sort of *see* **sort of**

kith/kin These plural nouns are often paired in the phrase *kith and kin.* Separately, *kith* means "nearby friends or neighbors" and *kin* means "relatives; members of one's own clan." *Kin* often appears on its own <I'd

like you to meet some more of my *kin*>, but *kith* now comes up almost exclusively in the phrase *kith and kin*

kneeled/knelt Both *kneeled* and *knelt* serve interchangeably as past tense and past participle of the verb *kneel* <She *kneeled* before me> <He *knelt* at the altar>

knit/knitted The past tense and past participle of the verb *knit* can be either *knit* or *knitted* <He had this entire outfit *knit* for himself> <She *knitted* her hands in front of her as she spoke>

knot While there's generally no confusion about tying rope into *knots,* the nautical sense of *knot* can tie some people up. On a ship *knot* means "nautical mile per hour," which means speed is expressed simply in *knots,* not in *knots per hour* <We were really booming along, going at about twenty *knots*>

knows/nose *see* **nose**

laboratory/lavatory A *laboratory* is "a place for scientific experimentation" <Dr. Frankenstein's *laboratory* is on the tour itinerary>. A *lavatory* is "a sink," "a washroom," or, in its most common usage, "a bathroom" <The only relief he had all day was when he finally found a *lavatory*>

laconic/sardonic/sarcastic *see* **sardonic**

laden/loaded To be *laden* is to be "weighed down" either literally <The trapper's mule was *laden* with pelts> or figuratively <She was *laden* with cares>. *Loaded* is either the past tense of the verb *load,* meaning "placed on or in" <The dockworkers *loaded* the ship with grain> or an adjective that can mean "having a load" <a *loaded* vehicle>, "tricky or deceitful" <a *loaded* statement>, or "drunk" <He's *loaded* every time I see him>

lady/woman *Lady* is the correct term in some references to the Virgin Mary <our *Lady* of mercy> and when talking about women with titles or knighthood in Britain <Lord and *Lady* Chamberlain>, in both cases taking a capital *L*. Most dictionaries claim that *lady* can be used as "a courteous reference to a woman," but it is considered disparaging and offensive by many women and men because of its connotations of gentility, inexperience with the world, and inability to cope <*Ladies* have no business coming into a place such as this>. The movement toward equal status between the sexes has led concerned, courteous people to use *woman* in almost all references to female human beings

laid/lain/lay/lied The past tense and past participle of *lay,* "to put down," is *laid* <We *laid* down our guns> <She was *laid* to rest> <He *laid* his bet on the table>. The past participle, or passive past tense, of *lie,* "to be horizontal," is *lain* <I had *lain* still all night listening to him breathe>, and its active past tense is *lay* <I *lay* beneath a blanket of stars that night>. The past and past participle of *lie* "to tell an untruth" is *lied* <He has *lied* about his previous employment, and now he *lied* about this job> *see* **lay/lie**

larceny/theft/robbery/burglary *see* **burglary**

large/big *see* **big**

last/latter Something that's *last* is "the final one of a series" <Here come John, Apple, and Sarah, and Bret comes *last*>. *Latter* is used to refer to "the second of two" <Meet Sarah and Bret, the *latter* being the one who isn't pregnant>. While *latter* is sometimes used to mean "the last of three or more," this is not accepted by most wordsmiths. It leads to confusion and is better handled by the terms *last-named* or *last.* In some instances *latter* can be confusing even when used with only two subjects <Apple and John and Sarah and Bret, the *latter* having lived next door>. If the use of *latter* could make the meaning unclear, repeat the name or rewrite the sentence instead <Apple and John and Sarah and Bret, the second couple having lived next door>

laudable/laudatory Both words have to do with praise, but they apply very differently. *Laudable* means "praiseworthy" and describes something that should be praised <Her *laudable* testimony, made at great personal risk, put him away for life>. *Laudatory* is "of or expressing praise" and describes words or actions that praise someone or something <The DA's *laudatory* remarks about the witness made him feel great>

lawyer/attorney/barrister/solicitor *see* **barrister**

lay/lie Two verbs with different meanings, *lay* and *lie* are often mistakenly interchanged. *Lay* means "to put down or place" and refers to things that are indicated <*Lay* the book on a shelf> <I wouldn't *lay* that gun by the fire if I were you>. *Lie* means "to remain horizontal" or "to assume a horizontal position, recline" <He hates to *lie* on concrete>. The phrase *now I lay me down to sleep* means "I place myself down to sleep"; once placed, however, someone could ask me, "How can you *lie* there like that?" *see* **laid/lain/lay/lied**

lead/leaden *Leaden* is the older form of the adjective meaning "made or consisting of lead" and is preferred by some, but *lead* is also completely acceptable in this sense and is in some cases preferred <a *lead* pipe> <a *leaden* capsule>

leak/leek A *leak* is "something that allows something else to get out" <The president complained about the *leak* that let secret escapades become public knowledge> <Once we got a *leak* in the pipe we knew we needed a plumber>. A *leek* is "an herb" used in cooking <Make a soup of potatoes and *leeks*>

leapt/leaped Either term is correct for the past tense or past participle of *leap,* "to jump, bound, spring" <He *leapt* from bed> <She *leaped* from the car just before it crashed>

leave alone/let alone Only in phrases with *alone* in the sense "keep from disturbing" are *leave* and *let* allowed to substitute for each other <*Leave* me *alone* and I'll do nothing at all> <If you'd *let* her *alone* she'd get the job done>. *Let alone* is also used to mean "or even, much less" <He can't read, *let alone* write>, a sense not indicated by *leave alone. Let* by itself is also the only choice for "allow" or "permit" <*Let* us get on with it> <Won't you *let* me kiss you?>

lectern/podium A *lectern* is "a stand that supports a speaker's notes or books or the speaker him- or herself" <She held tight to the *lectern* to keep her hands from flapping wildly as she spoke>. A *podium* is "the platform on which a speaker stands" <Won't you come up on the *podium* and address the group?>

legalize/decriminalize *see* **decriminalize**

legation/delegation Both terms describe people who represent others, but that's as far as the similarities go. A *legation* is "a diplomatic mission to a foreign country that ranks below an embassy" <The U.S. *legation* was snubbed by the Mozambican leader>. A *delegation* is "an officially appointed or elected group of representatives" <IBM's *delegation* at the conference>

legible/readable *see* **readable**

legislation/legislature *Legislation* is "the act of making laws" or "proposed laws being considered by an elected body" <*Legislation* outlawing peanut butter was widely condemned by third-graders across the state>. A *legislature* is "the body authorized to make laws" <Our state's *legislature* only meets for one month a year>. *Legislation* is what's adopted by a *legislature*

legitimize/legitimatize/legitimate All three words are interchangeable and have the meaning "to make lawful, justified, and acceptable" <*legitimize* her presence in the room> <*legitimatize* a bastard child by legally adopting him> <Why try to *legitimate* owning seventeen cars?>. *Legitimize* is the more euphonious of the three and the more commonly used

lend/loan/borrow Both *lend* and *loan* mean "to give temporarily" <Please *lend* me your sweater> <I like to *loan* out my books>, although some consider *loan* to be substandard as a verb and fit only for use as a noun <He took out a *loan* from his mother>. While *loan* has a long history as a verb, quibblers may object if it appears in more formal writing. *Borrow* is "to take temporarily" <She'd be happy to *borrow* the Porsche>, a sense for which *lend* and *loan* are often incorrectly used, especially in speech

lengthy/long These two are to some extent synonymous, meaning "extending in length, time, number, or size" <a *lengthy* field> <a *long* list of things to do>. In general use, however, *lengthy* is applied to senses of time <a *lengthy* and arduous board meeting> <*lengthy* debate> and *long* to distance, physical dimensions, and quantity <a *long* book> <a *long* way to Tipperary>

lenience/leniency *Lenience* is just an alternate form of *leniency,* "the state of being tolerant and forgiving" <He learned *lenience* at seminary> <Her *leniency* allowed him to remain in the classroom despite his disruptive remarks>. While both are correct, *leniency* is more commonly used

lent/loaned *Lent* is the past tense of *lend,* and *loaned* is the past tense of *loan,* both meaning "to have given temporarily." But because *loan* as a verb is not universally accepted, *loaned* is less frequently used than *lent*

less/fewer *see* **fewer**

levy/levee A *levy* is "a tax" or "a draft for military service" <It's a wonder they haven't put a *levy* on walking>; it can also be a verb "to tax" or "to draft." A *levee* is commonly used to mean "a dike or earthen embankment" <We spent the day on the *levee* skipping stones across the water>, although it can also mean "a reception given by a distinguished or royal person upon arising from bed" or "a formal reception" <The king, still in his nightshirt and looking kind of rumpled, greeted us as we arrived for the *levee*>

liable/libel *Liable* means "accountable, responsible" <Parents are *liable* for the actions of their children> or "likely" <We're not *liable* to show up at your party>. *Libel* is "a defamatory statement" <The truth should be an adequate defense against *libel*> or, as a verb, "to defame" *see* **accountable/liable/responsible, likely/apt/liable**

liaison There is a tendency in modern American speech to make a verb of anything even if it doesn't move. Such is the case with *liaison,* a noun that means "a close relationship or sexual affair" <We began our *liaison* innocently enough> or "communication" <in charge of *liaison* between officers and enlisted personnel>. It cannot and does not serve as a verb, either in the form "to liaison" or the even more offensive "to liaise." If a verb is needed, *relate, communicate,* and *make love* are terms that will serve the purpose in acceptable English

libel/slander Both *slander* and *libel* are "defamatory statements," but in legal use, *slander* is "an oral statement that defames and damages another's reputation" <She claimed that *slander* was her opponent's only recourse during the debate>, and *libel* is "written, published material that defames and damages another's reputation" <Just because the article makes you look like a louse doesn't mean they're guilty of *libel*>

lie/lay *see* **lay**

lied/laid/lain/lay *see* **laid**

lighted/lit Either word is acceptable as the past tense of *light* <He *lighted* a cigarette> <Her face *lit* up>

like/as *Like* can be used without argument as a preposition meaning "in the manner of" <She dances *like*

Isadora Duncan>, and *as* can be used without argument as a conjunction meaning "in the manner" <She dances *as* a dancer of her caliber ought to dance>. Heated debate begins, however, when *like* is used as a conjunction <Winston tastes good *like* a cigarette should>. *Like* has been used this way for centuries, and by all manner of reputable authors, so this use can be defended. But use of *like* as a conjunction will require defense, because it will be attacked by concerned linguaphiles. The easiest solution is to use *as* when "in the manner" could substitute and to reserve *like* for prepositional connections between words, phrases, or sentences that could be served by "in the manner of"

likely/apt/liable All three words are attached to the word *to* and used to mean "in a position," but there are shades of variation between them. *Likely* is the correct choice to indicate simple probability <We're *likely* to go to the concert>. *Apt* implies a natural tendency <He's *apt* to cry at weddings>. And *liable* is used when the connotation of risk or adversity is desired <Taking potshots at passing patrol cars is *liable* to get you in deep trouble>

limit/delimit In its verb senses, *limit* means "to set boundaries," whether physical or metaphorical <Writers *limit* themselves to what can be described in words>, "to restrict" <*limit* speed to thirty-five miles per hour>, or "to decrease" <*limit* power>. To *delimit* (or less frequently, *delimitate)* is "to set boundaries" in a literal, physical sense <After the war, the boundaries of East and West Germany were *delimited* by the Soviets and the U.S.>

limp/limpid As an adjective, *limp* means "not stiff," "tired," or "weak" <a *limp* character incapable of standing up for himself>. The adjective *limpid* means "clear" <a *limpid* description of a complex process>, "transparent" <a *limpid* pond>, or "serene" <the *limpid* state of mind derived from daily headstands>

linage/lineage *Linage* is a word used mostly in printing and publishing; it's "the number of lines" <The editorial *linage* for our fall issue is way down>. *Lineage* means "heritage" or "line of descent" <My own *lineage* dates back to seventeenth-century England>

line/queue *see* **queue**

lint/dust *Lint* is "linen fleece," "hairs carried by cotton seeds," or most commonly, "fuzz" <My dress coat seems to pick up *lint* everywhere I go>. *Dust* is "fine particles" <gold *dust*> <The *dust* piles up so quickly the maid just can't keep up>

literally Here is a word that has come to mean the opposite of what it means. *Literally* is "actually; in a literal way" <There was *literally* a foot of snow on the ground when we awoke>. But it often means "virtually, seemingly," and when this sense is used consciously for emphasis and the context isn't formal, it is generally acceptable <With all she's got to do she could *literally* work forever> *see* **virtually**

liven/enliven Both words mean "to make lively, awake, and excited," and can be used interchangeably. The only difference is that *liven* is often used with *up* <You've got to *liven up* this place, paint the walls or

something>, while *enliven* stands alone <He'll *enliven* the party just by being there>

livid Little wonder there's confusion about the meaning of *livid.* It can be "bruised" <the *livid* welts she'd show us after a beating>, "ashen" <You look *livid,* like you've just seen a ghost>, "angry" <I get *livid* just thinking about that fat pig's attitude toward me>, or "reddish" <He turns *livid,* embarrassed until his ears are crimson-hued>. The only way to avoid confusion is to be sure the context makes clear what sense is being used

load/lode *Load* can be "cargo" <Get that *load* on board the ship>, "a weight" <Looks like she's carrying a heavy *load*>, "power output or consumption" <a two-megawatt *load*>, or as a plural, "lots" <He made *loads* of creamed corn>; in the phrase *get a load of* it means "take a look at" <Get a *load* of that ugly guy with the enormous belly>; and as slang it's "enough liquor to get drunk" <She drank a *load* last night, believe me>. *Lode* is simply "a deposit of ore" <We struck a huge *lode* of uranium> or "a large supply" <He had a *lode* of reefer stashed away>; *lode* is also the spelling used in the phrase *mother lode,* "the main supply"

loaded/laden *see* **laden**

loaned/lent *see* **lent**

loath/loathe *Loath,* the adjective, means "not willing" <I'm *loath* to take on a new project while this one is unfinished>. *Loathe,* the verb, means "despise, hate" <I *loathe* working during the World Series>

locale/locality/place Small gradations of meaning separate these three. In their confusable senses, a *locale* is "where something happens," "a site" <The demonstration will take place at a new *locale* this year, in front of the mayor's home>; a *locality* is "a place in relation to other objects," "a neighborhood or region" <This *locality* has a more neighborly feel to it>; and a *place* is "a particular point or area of space," "a building or home," or "a city or village" <This *place* gives me the creeps>

lonely/lonesome *Lonely* and *lonesome* are synonymous in the senses "sad from being by oneself" <I'm feeling mighty *lonesome*> and "without company" <a *lonely* village high up the mountain>. They each have other senses too. *Lonely* can mean "devoid of people" <It's hard to find a *lonely* street in New York> or "able to induce sadness" <a *lonely* afternoon>. *Lonesome* carries the additional meanings "isolated" <going down that long, *lonesome* highway> and "self" <I'm going by my lonesome, if need be>

long/lengthy *see* **lengthy**

loosen/unloose/unloosen These three share just about the same meanings: "to relax," "to make loose," "to remove restrictions," and "to make less strict." *Loosen* often appears with *up* in the senses "to relax" and "to make less strict"

loquacious Being *loquacious* has nothing to do with elegance of speech. It means "wordy" or "talkative" <The *loquacious* speaker went on for so long I fell asleep twice>

lunch/luncheon *Lunch* is "a light meal eaten around noon." A *luncheon* is "a formal meal eaten around noon that includes a meeting or the honoring of a guest" <We

thought this was to be a *luncheon,* but it turned out to be a brown-bag *lunch* instead>

luxuriant/luxurious For the most part, *luxuriant* is used to mean "bountiful," "abundant," or "rich and varied" <a *luxuriant* undergrowth found in tropical climes> <a *luxuriant* variety of stunningly beautiful women>. *Luxuriant* can also be synonymous with *luxurious,* which means "easy and comfortable" <a *luxurious* life, with servants to wait on us hand and foot>, "expensive and superior in quality" <*luxurious* automobiles like the Rolls-Royce>, or "self-indulgent" <a *luxurious* hour rolling in the bubble bath with my rubber ducky>

lyric/lyrical These two adjectives are completely interchangeable. Either can mean "appropriate for being put to music," "operatic," "intensely emotional" <a *lyric* story that brings a tear to your eye>, or "happily unrestrained" <The *lyrical* party lasted all night>

macabre/bizarre Something *macabre* is "about death" <a *macabre* course in the history of forensic medicine>, "gruesome" <the *macabre* scene that followed a VC raid on a village>, or "horrifying" <a *macabre* movie that makes you wish you were home in bed>. *Bizarre* means "extremely strange" <*Bizarre* costumes appear in Greenwich Village even when it's not Halloween>

mad/crazy *Mad* and *crazy* are synonymous in senses where they mean "insane" <Hitler was *mad*>, "unrestrained" <We all got *crazy* and started taking off our clothes>, "enthusiastic" <I'm *mad* for these new candies>, "wild" <Once our clothes were off things started to get a little *crazy*>, or "frantic" <I started to get *mad* from the anxiety>

madam/madame Both words are polite ways of addressing women, but they are used differently. *Madam,* with the stress on the first syllable, is used without a first or last name <Excuse me, *madam,* I was wondering if you knew where the park is>, with a last name or title <*Madam* President>, with *the* to signify the female head of a household <I'd like you to meet the *madam*>, or to mean "the head of a house of prostitution" <Dolly Parton plays the *madam* in the film version of *The Best Little Whorehouse in Texas*>. *Madame,* with the stress on the second syllable, is used as a rough equivalent for *Mrs.* when addressing or introducing married women from non–English-speaking countries <I'd like to meet *Madame* de Beauvoir>

maddening/madding *Maddening* means "infuriating" <Waiting for trains that are canceled two hours later is *maddening*> or "inducing craziness" <Living on the streets can be *maddening* even to those who start out sane>. *Madding,* an obsolete word known only from the title *Far from the Madding Crowd,* means "frenzied"

magic/magical As an adjective, *magic* has the same meanings as *magical,* namely "having to do with magic" <a *magical* ability to pull elephants from people's ears>, "endowed with apparently supernatural powers" <a *magic* ability to silence a boisterous crowd>, or "inducing a spell-like feeling" <the *magical* cartoons of Max Fleischer>. *Magic,* of course, is also a noun, which *magical* is not

majority/plurality A *majority* is "more than half, most" <The *majority* of human beings are women> <win a *majority* of convention delegates' votes>. In the voting sense, a *plurality* is "more votes than any other candidate receives" or "the most votes in a contest of three or more candidates wherein no one gets more than half the votes cast" <It's possible to win a *majority* of electoral votes while getting only a *plurality* of the popular vote>. *Plurality* also means "the number of votes by which one candidate outpolls another" <win by a *plurality* of a thousand votes, five thousand to four thousand>

make/makes In general use, the difference between *make* and *makes* is readily apparent: I *make,* you *make,* he, she, or it *makes,* we *make,* they *make,* everyone or anyone *makes,* and so on. But when the verb appears in an informal mathematical expression, its number is hard to pin down. Is it "two plus three *makes* five" or "two plus three *make* five?" The subject in the example is *three,* which can be construed as singular, taking *makes,* or it can be the plural "three things," taking *make.* In short, either one is correct, depending on how you look at it *see* **is/are**

male/man *Male* is a classifying term that applies to humans, pigs, geese, and flowers, meaning "one that fertilizes female ova or organs." When speaking or writing of human beings, unless a good reason for classifying exists it's best to use *man* to describe male human beings <Steve's the only *man* in this year's group> <*Men* have certain needs>. If *male* is used, the correct counterpart is *female,* not *woman* <three *males* and a *female*> *see* **female/woman**

malfeasance/misfeasance/nonfeasance Another entanglement in the world of legal talk. *Malfeasance* is "wrongdoing, especially when illegal or constituting official misconduct" <If Reagan had admitted knowledge of a guns-for-hostages swap, it would have been an admission of *malfeasance*>. *Misfeasance* is "the carrying out of a legal and proper act in an illegal or improper manner" <Sexual intercourse between married men and women becomes *misfeasance* when done on the steps of city hall>. *Nonfeasance,* a word that is used less frequently outside legal circles than the *mal-* and *mis-* forms, means "inaction; the failure to do what should be done" <Although *malfeasance* could not be proved against Reagan in the Iran-contra scandal, he was certainly guilty of *nonfeasance*>

malign/impugn To *malign* is "to speak misleadingly about," whether on purpose or not <Some feel Judge Bork was *maligned* in confirmation hearings>. To *impugn* is "to attack; to argue against" <Whether or not his positions were misrepresented, there's little doubt Bork's suitability for the Supreme Court was *impugned*> *see* **benign/malign, impugn/imply**

mall/maul A *mall* is "a public area that serves as a walkway," "a strip that separates two roads," "a usually enclosed suburban shopping area," or "an open-air urban shopping area." *Mall* is also a variant spelling of *maul,* which is the preferred spelling for the noun meaning "a hammer for driving wedges or splitting wood" and for the verb that means "to beat viciously" <He was *mauled* by a gang of thugs>

mandatory/compulsory *Mandatory* and *compulsory* both mean "required, not optional" <*Mandatory* drug tests are becoming the norm> <*Compulsory* fitness tests are the only way of measuring everyone's level of physical achievement>. *Compulsory* also can mean "coercive" <The stiff fines will have a *compulsory* effect on others>

mantle/mantel A *mantle* is "a cloak or hood" or "something that covers" <under the *mantle* of dark-

ness>; capitalized, it's the name of the great Yankees slugger of the nineteen fifties and sixties. *Mantle* is also a variant spelling of *mantel,* "the structure surrounding a fireplace, especially the shelf above a fireplace" <Keep your trophies on the *mantel*>. To avoid the appearance of misuse, it's best to use *mantel* around the fireplace

marginal/minimal/small *Marginal* means "at the edge of" <*marginal* consciousness>, "in the margins of" <*marginal* notes>, or "close to the least acceptable" <*marginal* profits>. *Minimal* is "the least possible or acceptable" <*Minimal* effort produces *minimal* results>. *Small* is used to describe things that are "little in value or number" <Even a major event can pull in only a *small* profit>. In a hierarchy, *marginal* is more than *minimal,* and both are interchangeable with, though more specific than, *small*

masterful/masterly Both *masterful* and *masterly* can be used to mean "showing the attributes or skills of a master" <a *masterful* performance> <a *masterly* piece of writing>. *Masterful* alone also has the senses "overbearing in acting as a master" <his boastful, swaggering, *masterful* approach to leadership> and "suited to being a master" <She's *masterful* when she can choose her own lieutenants>

material/materiel *Material* is "anything physical; stuff, matter" <Sweep up whatever *material* you find on the sidewalk>, "cloth" <He embroidered some plain *material*>, or as an adjective, "nonspiritual" <We're living in a *material* world>. *Materiel* is mostly used to mean "guns, ammunition, and other military supplies" <a planeload of *materiel* on its way to Iran>, although it can be "the equipment and supplies of any organization" <The Art Students League had very little *materiel*>

may/can *see* **can**

maybe/may be The single word *maybe* is an adverb that means "perhaps" <*Maybe* I'll go to the store>; it can only appear in sentences that contain a verb, such as *go* in the example. As two words, *may be* acts as a verb phrase indicating "possible existence or action" <I *may be* going to the store> <It *may be* a yes-or-no situation>

mayoral/mayoralty *Mayoral* is an adjective meaning "of or about the head of a city's government" <awaiting *mayoral* action on the proposal>. *Mayoralty,* a noun, means "the position of mayor; the term of a mayor's stay in office" <Koch's *mayoralty* may just last forever>

me/myself Most people in most situations know when to use *me* <Excuse *me*> <Do you mean *me?*> and when *myself* <I can't find it *myself*> <By *myself* I'm totally peaceful>. But as with *I* and *me,* problems arise when self-reference is needed for the second of a pair of pronouns. People use *myself* because of the mistaken notion that *me* can never be right in any such situation, or in the belief that *myself* is simply a more important way of saying "me" <The notion of my wife and *myself* sharing a single bed was ridiculous> <Invited guests included the duchess of Windsor and *myself*>. Although such phraseology is often heard, it's incorrect in formal writing. The right choice in such situations is *me* *see* **I/me**

mean/median/average A *mean,* in the sense in which it might be confused with *median* and *average,* is "a middle point between two extremes" <Today's high

temperature was 60 degrees, the low was 30, and the *mean* was 45>. In another sense, *mean* is synonymous with *average:* "a figure gotten by adding together a set of figures and dividing by the number of figures added" <The *mean* of 1, 3, 4, 6, and 11 is 5>; the second sense is more properly called an *arithmetic mean.* A *median* is "the figure in a set that has an equal number of figures above and below it" <The *median* of 1, 3, 4, 6, and 11 is 4>

meaningful In its proper sense, *meaningful* means "having meaning; significant" <A *meaningful* statement about how to reduce the budget deficit would be most welcome> <She gave a *meaningful* look to her counterpart, who knew at once her intentions>. Alas, careless use of this word is in evidence on almost a daily basis, with meanings like "impressive" <He gave a truly *meaningful* lecture> or "sexually and intellectually worthwhile" <a *meaningful* relationship>. Such meanings may one day render *meaningful* meaningless, and should be avoided

media/medias/mediums Both *media* and *mediums* are acceptable plural forms of *medium;* they mean "mass communications outlets" <print, radio, and TV *media*> <Print and telecommunications are two such *mediums*>. The singular form is *medium* <Newspapers are one *medium*>. Despite increasing use of *media* as a singular noun <The *media* is interested in nothing but sensationalism>, it is not accepted or correct. And once it's clear that *media* is plural, the absurdity of *medias* becomes obvious

melted/molten Something that has been "rendered liquid by heat" can be said to have *melted* <They *melted*

the gold bars>. *Melted* can also serve as an adjective meaning "in a liquid state because heat has been applied" <*melted* silver>, a sense shared by *molten* <*Molten* steel spilled out of the vessels>. *Molten* also means "glowing and giving off heat" <the *molten* logs on the fire>. *Melted* can be used in more figurative senses like "dissolved" <The candy *melted* in my mouth>, "merged" <He *melted* into her arms>, or "made emotionally soft" <My heart *melted* when I saw that puppy>

memento/momento Perhaps because it has been misspelled so often, some dictionaries give *momento* as a variant of *memento,* "a remembrance or reminder; a souvenir" <We hope this watch will serve as a *memento* of your years of valued service>. The proper spelling is *memento*

mercenary/missionary Some cynics might suggest these words are interchangeable, but they're not. A *mercenary* is "one whose incentive is money, especially a soldier or adventurer" <Are the contras really patriotic Nicaraguans or merely profiteering *mercenaries?*>. A *missionary* often serves in overseas locales but is "one who represents a religious organization by evangelizing and doing good works" <After years in Africa as a *missionary* he moved to Switzerland and became a hermit>

merry-go-round/carousel *see* **carousel**

meteor/meteorite A *meteor* is "a streak of light in the sky caused by a piece of celestial debris moving through the earth's atmosphere" or "a piece of celestial debris that is vaporized in the atmosphere" <Maine and South Dakota are good places to watch *meteors*> <A *meteor* shower is an impressive sight>. When one of these chunks of debris survives its trip through the atmosphere and lands on earth, it is a *meteorite* <a small trove of *meteorites* housed in a museum>

miasma Sometimes thought to mean "a lot," *miasma* is actually "an atmosphere" in several literal and figurative senses. Historically it was "a poisonous vapor in the atmosphere that causes disease and death" <In 1986 a *miasma* belched forth from a volcanic lake in Africa, killing villagers in their sleep>. In modern use, it mostly describes "a heavy vapor or smoke" <the *miasma* of pot smoke in the dorm room> or "a debilitating atmosphere or environment" <escaping the *miasma* of New York's Lower East Side>

millenary/millinery A *millenary* is "a thousand things" or "a thousand years; a millenium" <In a few short years, the third *millenary* A.D. will be upon us>. *Millinery* is "women's hats" <Bloomie's carries the finest Italian *millinery*>. The distinction in spelling and meaning will become important as the year A.D. 2001 approaches

minimal/minimum Either word can be used as an adjective meaning "the smallest possible number or amount" <*minimal* price increases> <*minimum* effort>. *Minimum* also functions as a noun <There is a *minimum* below which we cannot drop our standards> *see* **nominal/minimal**

minimize/reduce To *minimize* is "to make as small as possible" <You can *minimize* emotional risks by staying home alone>. To *reduce* is "to decrease" <You can *reduce* emotional risks by meeting only those people your friends already know>. When something is reduced as much as possible, it has been minimized

minister/priest/reverend/pastor/rector *see* **reverend**

minuscule As a noun, *minuscule* is "a lowercase letter" <The calligrapher showed him how to make *minuscules* and majuscules>. When used as an adjective it means "very small, tiny" <Since she's on a diet she can only have a *minuscule* amount of cake>. In either case, the word is spelled with a *u,* like *minus,* and not with an *i,* like *mini*

misfeasance/nonfeasance/malfeasance *see* **malfeasance**

mitigate/militate To *mitigate* is "to soothe, moderate, make milder and less hostile" <She *mitigated* his anger by sending a dozen roses>. To *militate,* from the same root as *military,* is just the opposite, "to fight or have force," and is almost always used with *against* <The power of the dollar *militated* against the striking NFL players>

mongoloid/cretin In the most common usage—meaning "stupid, idiotic, loutish person"—*cretin* is the correct choice. A *mongoloid* is "one affected by Down's Syndrome," and a *cretin* is "one affected by a severe thyroid deficiency," both problems resulting in mental deficiency. But while *cretin* is an acceptable term for someone who acts stupidly, *mongoloid* is not

monkish/monastic *Monkish* means "having to do with monks" <His *monkish* life includes five hours of reading before dawn>. *Monastic* is "having to do with monasteries" <The unfurnished house look downright

monastic>, although since monks live in monasteries, *monastic* can also mean *monkish*

monkey/simian/ape *see* **simian**

monotonic/monotonous Both *monotonic* and *monotonous* can mean "having a single unvarying tone" <a *monotonic* speaker> <a *monotonous* clarinet solo>. *Monotonic* has a mathematically oriented sense, "remaining constant as an independent variable changes." *Monotonous* can also be used in the sense "boringly repetitious" <the *monotonous* study of Latin inflections>

moral/morale As an adjective, *moral* can mean "right and just" <a *moral* stand against the forces of evil> or "likely but unproven" <a *moral* certainty>. *Moral* can also serve as a noun with the senses "a lesson in right and wrong" <TV shows entertain but don't offer a *moral*> or in its plural form, "codes of conduct" <Students need *morals,* not beatings>. *Morale* is always a noun that can apply to individuals or groups and carries the meaning "willingness, cheerfulness, and dedication to carrying out a task at hand" <After losing thirty-nine straight games, the Columbia football team's *morale* was surprisingly high>. The two can always be told apart aurally because the stress is on the first syllable in *moral* and on the second syllable in *morale* *see* **ethical/moral**

moron/idiot Both terms apply to the feebleminded but differ in the degree of feeblemindedness. A *moron* is "a person with a mental age of between eight and twelve years, one who is the least mentally deficient of the type," while an *idiot* is "a person with a mental age of up to three years, one who is the most mentally deficient." Of course, these words are not used only to technically define the feebleminded, and their more popular uses are somewhat less differentiated. *Moron* can mean "a very stupid person," "an oaf," or "a fool." *Idiot* is "a silly person," "a fool," or "a blockhead." Either can be used by one sibling to describe another

mortician/undertaker/funeral director *see* funeral director

mortise/mortar A *mortise* (sometimes spelled *mortice)* is a construction term meaning "a hole that is usually rectangular, cut to fit a projection from another piece" <This *mortise* is too small to take that tenon>. It can also serve as a verb meaning "to join by a mortise and tenon" or "to cut a mortise," and in printing it means "a hole cut in a plate to insert type" or "to cut a hole in a plate." *Mortar* is also used in construction; it's "a cement used in masonry and plastering" <We slapped *mortar* in the cracks hoping no one would notice them> or, as a verb, "to hold in place or plaster with a cement." *Mortar* is also "a vessel in which grinding is done" <*mortar* and pestle>, and "a cannon"

Moslem/Muslim "A follower of Islam" is sometimes called a *Moslem* and sometimes a *Muslim.* The form preferred by the followers of Islam themselves is *Muslim,* which makes it the more appropriate choice. Members of the Nation of Islam, the so-called Black Muslims, insist *Muslim* is the only acceptable spelling

most/almost In formal writing it's best to use *almost* when the meaning is "nearly" <*Almost* everyone came to our party>. The abbreviated version *most* is widely accepted in speech and less so in writing. It should be restricted to modifying *all, any,* and *every,* or compounds beginning with them like *always, anybody,* or *everyone* <She *most* always gets here before seven> <*Most* anything could be used for a marker>

move/opportunity/gambit *see* **gambit**

multilateral/bilateral/unilateral *see* **bilateral**

must/need When responding to an inquiry about whether or not something is required, *must* (or *have to*) is correct for a positive answer <Do you have to go? Yes, I *must*> and *need* (or again *have to)* is the right choice when the answer is no <Must you wear that suit? No, I *needn't*>

mutual/common In the sense in which they're confused, *mutual* is frequently used to describe something each person has individually; it means "of each for the other or others" <*mutual* affection>. *Common* is "shared; belonging to all together" <a *common* bathroom>. Either word can be used when the meaning is "joint" <our *mutual* self-interest> <our *common* self-sufficiency> *see* **reciprocal/mutual**

myself/me *see* **me**

N

nabob A word for which we can thank disgraced Vice President Spiro Agnew, who placed it in the limelight by using the phrase "nattering *nabobs* of negativism." Agnew did nothing to make its meaning clear, however, and many took it be equivalent to *idiot.* Not so. A *nabob* is either "an important or wealthy person" <Mike Wallace, Katharine Graham, and the other media *nabobs*> or "a governor in India during the Mogul empire"

naked/nude In the sense "without clothing of any sort," *naked* and *nude* are interchangeable <a *naked* man and a *nude* woman performing lewd and lascivious acts>. *Naked* and *nude* are also synonyms that mean "lacking covering or vegetation" <*naked* trees>. *Naked* alone has the senses "undecorated" <a *naked* mantelpiece>, "undisguised" <*naked* lust>, and "unarmed" <went into the crooks' lair *naked,* without even a knife>. *Nude* can be used in legal circles to mean "lacking some necessary component" <a *nude* contract>

naught/aught *see* **aught**

nauseated/nauseous There is great debate among the experts about whether the adjectival sense "sick to the stomach or disgusted" can properly be represented by *nauseous,* or if *nauseated* is the only correct form <I feel *nauseous*> <He feels *nauseated*>. There is no disagreement that *nauseous* means "causing nausea or loathing" <a *nauseous* performance that chased most of the audience away by intermission>. Some feel that *nauseous* should be left to serve that sense alone, and that *nauseated* should be the only correct way of saying "feeling nausea or loathing." That separation of duties has historically been correct, but times change and language changes. *Nauseous* has in recent years been widely used to mean "feeling sick to the stomach or disgusted." While some fuddy-duddies may say it's wrong, and in strictly formal writing it is incorrect, it will pass unchallenged most of the time

near/nearly Either *near* or *nearly* can be used to mean "almost" <He turned up *nearly* dead from exhaustion>. *Near* also has the sense of "close to" <Stand *near* the wall>, which it doesn't share with *nearly*

nearsighted/shortsighted Either word is acceptable for the meaning "able to better see things that are closer" <so *nearsighted* he can't even see a wall until it's too late to keep from walking into it> <too *shortsighted* to drive without glasses>. *Shortsighted* also means "lacking prescience or prudence" <Her *shortsighted* grab for big bucks left her with an empty, meaningless life>

need/must *see* **must**

neither . . . nor/either . . . or *see* **either . . . or**

Netherlands/Holland *see* **Holland**

nevertheless/nonetheless These terms are interchangeable. They mean "however; regardless of that" <Although we have food, we are *nevertheless* without dinner until it's cooked> <He thought he'd be home that night. *Nonetheless,* he didn't get home all week>

nexus In recent years *nexus* has added a sense to its long-standing meanings "a connection" and "a group of connected things" <The *nexus* of decision-making includes the actors, the arena, and the outputs, Kodjoe tells us>. That new sense is "the center" <The *nexus* of our organization is actually the treasurer>, a sense that will certainly be decried by purists once they find out about it, but which has crept into the language so quickly and stealthily that it may become too firmly entrenched to do much about it. Until this meaning is more widely recognized, however, it's best to be cautious about using *nexus* to mean "center" in formal contexts

nice "Good," "pleasant," "refined," "upright," "hard to please," "discerning," "precise," "appropriate," "well-executed"—all are meanings of *nice.* If ever a word were overworked to the point where it becomes almost meaningless, this is it. *Nice* doesn't confuse so much as hide the true sense of what's being indicated and so should be avoided whenever possible

nocturnal/diurnal *see* **diurnal**

noisome/noisy From looking at them you could reasonably believe these words must be interchangeable, but they aren't. *Noisome* things bother your nose, *noisy* ones bother your ears. *Noisome* is "offensive, especially to the sense of smell" <Acrid, *noisome* smoke hung in the air> or "dangerous, unwholesome" <*noisome* urban slums unfit even for the rats that live there>. *Noisy,* of course, is "making loud sounds" or "having loud sounds" <a *noisy* room>

nominal/minimal When speaking of amounts, especially amounts of money, these two are virtually synonymous. *Nominal* means "small, insignificant" <She wanted to give it away, but we insisted on paying at least a *nominal* price>. *Minimal* is "the smallest possible, least" <Ten dollars is the *minimal* amount you should bring>. A *nominal* sum could be the *minimal* amount, or it could be slightly more than that *see* **minimal/minimum**

none is/none are Many believe that *none* means "no one" or "not one," and that it must take a singular verb. This is only right when *none* can be readily replaced by *no one* or *not one* <*None* of us *is* ready to leave> or when a singular noun follows *none* <*None* of the flatware *is* on the table>. *None* can also mean "not any" or "no people or things," and in these instances the verb should be plural <*None* of our friends *are* pleased with our decision> <*None are* more cheerful than the robins>. To decide which is correct in any given case, try substituting *not one* and *not any* for *none.* If *not one* makes sense, use *is;* if *not any* works, use *are*

nonfeasance/malfeasance/misfeasance *see* **malfeasance**

nor/or *Nor* is, of course, the conjunction that follows *neither* in a series of two or more negatives <Neither she *nor* I have ever been to Nicaragua>. *Nor* can also serve the same purpose when it appears without *neither* <He can't go, *nor* can his wife>. In instances where it's clear from the context that a negative sense is being continued, *or* can be used instead <She isn't interested, *or* doesn't think she is> <It's not reasonable *or* equitable to make such a move> *see* **either . . . or/neither . . . nor**

north/North *North* has a lowercase *n* when it is used to generally describe the direction <We went *north*> or to mean "zero degrees on a compass" <I knew we were going the wrong way, even though her compass read *north*>. The word is sometimes capitalized when it means "the northern part of the globe" <Scott explored the South, not the *North*>. *North* always has a capital *N* when referring to that part of the U.S. that formed the Union side of the Civil War <She lived all her life in Alabama without even once visiting the *North*> or a clearly defined region lying to the north in any country or region <When Mexicans talk about the *North,* they don't mean Tijuana>. When the term is not well established or the region is unfamiliar to most readers, *north* should be lowercased unless the writer carefully defines the region referred to by the capitalized term <The area from the river to the coast—the *North*—is sparsely populated>

northern/Northern As with *north, northern* is lowercased when used generally to mean "located toward the north" <the *northern* part of New York State, the Adirondacks> or "coming from the north" <a *northern* wind>. It's capitalized when referring to a place known as the North <Southerners know that *Northern* attitudes and

manners are more uptight> or the dialect spoken there <I can't understand *Northern* locution at all>

nose/knows A *nose* is "the projection in the middle of the face that covers and includes the nasal cavity" <I have a cold in my *nose*>. *Knows* is the third-person singular form of the verb *know,* "to have understanding and cognizance of" <He *knows* we're in here>. *Nose* has to do with *n*asal, *knows* with *know*ledge

notable/notorious Something is described as *notable* if it is positive in the sense "worthy of being known, remarkable, impressive" <She's a *notable* presence at those meetings she attends>. *Notorious,* on the other hand, is a negative word that means "widely known and ill-regarded" <a *notorious* criminal> <Reagan's *notorious* confrontational policies in developing countries>

not guilty/innocent *see* **innocent**

nude/naked *see* **naked**

number/amount *see* **amount**

O/oh *O* is very rarely used in modern writing or speech, but it should be kept distinct from *oh. O* is always capitalized and is used in direct, formal address <A toast to you, *O* mighty ocean> <*O* Lord above>. The more common *oh* has a capital *o* only when it starts a sentence, and serves as an interjection that acknowledges something <*Oh,* I get it now>, expresses surprise or amazement <And then, *oh,* what a shock we had>, or serves to call someone <*Oh,* waiter, another bottle of champagne>

oblige/obligate In the sense of "force to do or restrain from doing," where absolute compulsion is brought to bear, *oblige* and *obligate* are synonyms <I was *obliged,* under the terms of our agreement, to send her away><She was *obligated* to leave after she received the notice>. When the sense is "feel indebted or compelled" by moral, ethical, or social forces that are not compulsory, *oblige* is the right choice <I'm much *obliged* for your help> <He felt *obliged* to attend the meeting>

oblique/opaque *Oblique* has to do with lines and directions, *opaque* with transparency and color. In the senses in which they're confused, *oblique* means "indirect, evasive, misleading" <An *oblique* response to a simple, straightforward question>, and *opaque* means "incomprehensible" <enough double-talk to make the statement thoroughly *opaque*> or "thickheaded, stupid" <He was *opaque,* unresponsive, and apparently unable to understand>

oblivious/unaware Both *oblivious* and *unaware* mean "not cognizant." They differ in that *oblivious* is used with either *of* or *to* <*oblivious* of your surroundings> <*oblivious* to the noise>, but *unaware* is used only with *of* <*unaware* of how difficult writing can be>. *Oblivious* can also be used to mean "having no memory" <She was *oblivious* of her previous lives until reading about Shirley MacLaine>; although this used to be its only meaning, its "not cognizant" sense is now readily accepted

obscene/profane/vulgar Something *obscene* is "offensive, especially because it is lewd, indecent, and sexually arousing" <The public is fascinated by *obscene* photos showing celebrities in the nude>. A *profane* act or person is "offensive, especially because of disrespect or irreverence toward God or religion" <Fellini's *profane* attitude toward the Church>. Something *vulgar* is "offensive, especially because it is crude, excessively showy, or lacking in taste or manners" <a *vulgar* display that included offensive digestive noises and nasty remarks>. These senses can be kept separate, but they also spill into each other. Something *obscene* can also be *profane* <She wanted to fuck the pope>, and anything that is *obscene* or *profane* is almost certainly *vulgar* too

observance/observation In the sense "the act of watching," either term is correct <police *observance* of the reputed shooting gallery> <our lunchtime *observation* of all the good-looking men and women on the street>. *Observance* is also used to mean "the celebration of or compliance with a religious rite, legal requirement, or social custom" <*Observance* of Christmas transcends the Christians>. *Observation* has the added sense "a result or conclusion stemming from an act of watching" <Our *observations,* after having the place staked out for three weeks, include an instance of double-parking out front>

ocean/sea *see* **sea**

odd/oddly *Odd* is the adjective meaning "strange, weird, unusual" <an *odd* party> <The evening was *odd* enough> or, when used with a number, to indicate an approximation <forty-*odd* pieces>. *Oddly* is the adverb <Everyone at the party acted *oddly*> <The evening went *oddly*> <*Oddly* enough, we enjoyed it>. *Oddly* does sometimes appear as the first part of a compound adjective <*oddly* shaped rooms> <*oddly* synchronized audio and video tracks>, but it retains its adverbial form and function and is usually not hyphenated

odor/smell/stink The standard use of both *odor* and *smell* is with the meaning "scent; olfactory perception." They are generally interchangeable and have no connotations, good or bad <an unusual *odor*> <an unmistakable *smell*>. *Stink,* on the other hand, means "foul or sickening scent" <the permeating *stink* of a skunk>. In slang senses, however, *smell* and *stink* are synonymous verbs meaning "to be vile and contemptible" <She yelled, "You *stink,*" after I yelled, "You *smell*">

of/have Because of the sound of such contractions as *would've, could've,* and *should've, of* is turning up more and more frequently in place of *have* or *'ve.* "I *would of* gone to the store" or "I *could of* been a contender" are simply wrong, whatever the context

off/off of/off from Although widely used, especially in speech, the phrase *off of* is deemed unacceptable; *off* alone does the job <Get your feet *off* my couch> <She took her hat *off* her head>. Some dictionaries also prohibit *off from,* which can be incorrect in contexts like "Get your ring *off from* your finger," but which can also be acceptable in the sense "away and separated from" <He moved *off from* the crowd, heading along the deserted beach>

officious/official *Officious,* a much misunderstood and misused word, means "interfering; overly anxious to offer assistance" <Your *officious* attitude doesn't let us do anything ourselves> or, in diplomatic circles, "unofficial" <The attaché's *officious* comment does nothing to change our relations>. *Official* means "authorized" <an *official* NFL jacket> or "having to do with an office or position" <the *official* duties of the vice president>.

off-putting There are reputable dictionaries that accept the adjective *off-putting* as meaning "repellent, tending to put off" <her *off-putting,* highfalutin demeanor>. But something that's *off-putting* could be "offensive," "upsetting," or "in poor taste." Since the exact meaning is unclear, and the word itself is an awkward and unnecessary back formation from the phrase *to put off,* it's preferable to select a more precise adjective instead

oh/O *see* **O**

OK/O.K./okay Any of these forms can be used as a noun <Your proposal gets my *OK*>, a verb <I'll be happy to *O.K.* your report>, or as an adjective <an *okay* move> or adverb <she feels *OK* now>. This concise, clear term is acceptable in business writing, most speech, and a great many other contexts, although it does not belong in contracts, reports, deeds, or other formal documents

on/in *see* **in**

on/upon *see* **upon**

one another/each other *see* **each other**

one . . . one's/ . . . his or her/ . . . their In attempts to avoid sexist language, writers frequently resort to the pronoun *one,* "a person." They are then almost as frequently confused about which possessive to pair with it <*One* should always handle *one's* own dirty work> <*One* needs to deal with *his or her* own mistakes><*One* can respect *their* own record>. The only acceptable possessive is *one's; his, her, his or her,* or *their* are wrong. Of course, this can lead to some fairly cumbersome constructions <*One* can hardly help *one's* feelings, *one's* thoughts, or *one's* own past activities, no matter how much *one* tries>. In many instances, it's best to rewrite the sentence altogether, replacing *one* with a more specific reference <*Harry* can hardly help *his* feelings> or with the less unwieldy *people* <*People* can't control *their* own thoughts>

older/elder *see* **elder**

ongoing *Ongoing* can be used to mean "continuing," "progressing," or "active," but it is mostly used to make something that exists sound more important <Our *ongoing* project feeds and shelters the homeless>. The example is in no way improved by the presence of *ongoing.* The present tense tells the reader or listener that the project is indeed active. *Ongoing* only serves the purpose of cluttering up an otherwise readable sentence. It can always be left out with no adverse effect

on line/in line *see* **in line**

on purpose/purposefully/purposely *see* **purposely**

onto/on to/on *Onto* and *on* can serve more or less interchangeably as prepositions meaning "move toward" <She walked *onto* the stage> <He walked *on* the stage>, although *onto* is used more often in this sense. *Onto* and *on to* serve differently, however. *Onto* is again a preposition indicating motion toward something, but as separate words *on* is an adverb modifying the verb and *to* is a preposition <I went *on to* the next item on the agenda> <He always liked going *on to* new projects>

onward/onwards When modifying a verb, *onward* and *onwards* are interchangeable <We moved *onwards*> <She trundled *onward*>. As an adjective, only *onward* is acceptable <an *onward* march>. In general, *onward* is preferred in the U.S.

opportunity/gambit/move *see* **gambit**

opposite to/opposite from/opposite of/opposite than When *opposite* is an adjective it can be used with either *to* or *from* <Her plan is *opposite to* mine> <That's *opposite from* what he said>. As a noun, *opposite* is used only with *of* <I ended up doing the *opposite of* what I'd planned to do>. The phrase *opposite than* is never correct

opaque/oblique *see* **oblique**

op. cit./ibid. *see* ***ibid.***

oppugn/impugn *Oppugn* and *impugn* both mean "to call into question; to argue against," although *impugn* connotes that what is being argued against is false, while *oppugn* implies it is merely being opposed *see* **impugn/imply, malign/impugn**

Oprah/Opus Although they have never been seen together in public, there is little doubt that these words signify very different things. *Oprah* is the human talk-show host. *Opus* is a penguin (or possibly a puffin), a rock musician, and a known proponent of "penguin lust"

optimistic/hopeful *see* **hopeful**

optometrist/ophthalmologist/optician An *optometrist* is "one who tests eyesight and prescribes corrective lenses." An *opthalmologist* is "a medical doctor who specializes in diseases and disorders of the eye." And an *optician* is "one who makes or sells corrective lenses and eyeglasses"

or/nor *see* **nor**

oral/verbal Both *oral* and *verbal* mean "spoken," but other senses of *verbal* can make its meaning unclear. *Oral* pertains strictly to the mouth, so an *oral agreement* would be one made in speech, not in writing. *Verbal* has the additional senses "of or having to do with words," "literal," or "being concerned with words themselves instead of their meanings," so a *verbal agreement* could simply be one concerning words, such as a contract for a book. Unless the context makes the meaning absolutely clear, it's best to use *oral* when the meaning is "spoken"

ordinance/ordnance An *ordinance* is "a law, rule, or regulation" <We violated the municipal *ordinance* by parking on the wrong side of the street>. *Ordnance* is "ammunition and weaponry" or "heavy artillery" <A quick survey of U.S. *ordnance* found a ten percent shortage in ammunition supplies>

orient/orientate In the verb senses "to face toward the east" and "to place or adjust, especially in relation to other objects, events, or points on a compass," *orient* and *orientate* are synonyms, although it is a mystery why anyone would choose more syllables when fewer will do <Once I *oriented* myself I could get downtown> <He couldn't *orientate* himself in the woods even if he had a compass on a clear morning at sunrise>

Oriental/Asian Both words are used to mean "a person from Asia, or one whose ancestors are from Asia" <in Chinatown, where the *Orientals* live> <Most of the greengrocers are *Asians*>. Many people whose parents or grandparents came from China, Japan, Korea, or nearby countries prefer *Asian,* however, because of the perceived stereotypes associated with the term *Oriental*

ostensibly/ostentatiously *Ostensibly* means "apparently" <It was *ostensibly* the end of the show, so we were quite surprised when the cast reappeared at the back of the theater>. *Ostentatiously* means "showily" <He *ostentatiously* flashed a wrist dripping with designer watches>

our/ours *Our* is an adjective meaning "of or belonging to us"; as an adjective, it needs something to modify <*our* house> <*our* piece of work> <*our* and their forces combined>. *Ours* is a pronoun meaning "that or those belonging to us"; it stands alone without a noun or another pronoun <The house is *ours*> <the combination of their forces and *ours*>

out/out of When *out* is a preposition meaning "through," the preposition *of* is superfluous <fall *out* the window>. When the word describes motion away from something, and the something that's being moved away from is named, *of* should appear <She got *out of* the car> <The ball went *out of* sight, landing two blocks away>

outside/without *see* **without**

outstanding/exceptional/egregious *see* **egregious**

overlay/overlie Both *overlay,* as a verb, and *overlie* have the same basic sense, "to cover," but they apply differently. *Overlay* is generally used to mean "attach or place over" <*overlay* bare wood with linoleum>. *Overlie* is mostly used to mean "spread upon, existing over" <Snow *overlies* the cold winter landscape> *see* **lay/lie**

overlook/oversee To *overlook* is "to observe from a higher place" <The house *overlooks* the sea>, "to not observe, whether deliberately or not" <I'll *overlook* those stupid remarks>, and in the sense it shares with *oversee,* "to supervise" <The boss tries to *overlook* her

production line once in a while, but generally it's the manager who *oversees* our work>

overtone/undertone In the senses that do not have to do with color or music, *undertone* and *overtone* are approximately synonymous, meaning "suggestion, implication" <*overtones* of jealousy in an ostensibly pleasant greeting> <a sane facade with *undertones* of madness>

P

pachyderm Long used in the popular press as a substitute for *elephant,* a *pachyderm* is actually any of several thick-skinned, hoofed mammals, including the elephant, the rhinoceros, the pig, or the hippopotamus <A variety of *pachyderms* is on display at the zoo>

pair/pairs A *pair* is "a set of two" <He bought a new *pair* of shoes>. If more than one set is involved, *pairs* is the usual form <six *pairs* of mismatched socks>, although sometimes *pair* is used, especially in speech <three *pair* of gloves>

pair . . . is/ . . . are *Pair* can be a singular noun, taking the verb *is,* if the emphasis is on the set as a unit rather than the items making up the set <A *pair* of sturdy walking shoes *is* recommended>. When the emphasis is on the individuals comprising a pair, the word can be construed as plural, taking the verb *are* <That *pair are* as different as day and night, yet they remain together>

palate/palette/pallet The *palate* is "the roof of the mouth" or "the sense of taste" <Great culinary effort is wasted on those with no *palate*>; this word is the root of the term *palatable,* "tasty, enjoyable." "A board on which painters mix and hold pigments" is a *palette* <Picasso's *palette* held mostly blues at one point in his career>. A *pallet* is "a small, hard bed" <Make me a *pallet* on the floor> or "a portable storage platform" <We used fork-lifts to move the *pallets* from one end of the warehouse>

pamphlet/brochure *see* **brochure**

parameter/perimeter *Parameter* is a scientific term that has taken on the broader, more general senses "characteristic element" <Courage is one of this ball club's *parameters*>, "boundary" <Our explorations have yet to turn up the *parameters* of this property>, or "limit" <The department must not exceed its budgetary *parameter*>. The acceptability of these meanings is disputed by some authorities, who prefer *perimeter* when the meaning is "boundary" or "limit." In formal speech and writing, the universally accepted *perimeter* is the better choice

pardon/excuse Both terms are used for apologies <*Pardon* me for bumping into you> <*Excuse* me for burping at the table> and to indicate forgiveness <She *pardoned* his rudeness> <He *excused* her tardiness>. *Excuse* is also used in the sense "to allow an absence or exemption" <*excused* from jury duty>, while *pardon* has the specific sense "to forgive a criminal act for which guilt has been established" <Ford's *pardon* of Nixon made it quite clear that Nixon had broken the law>. The old differentiation in etiquette that called for using *excuse me* when manners lapsed and *pardon me* when requesting permission to leave is no longer applied

parricide/patricide *Parricide* is "the murder of one's mother, father, or other close relative" or "one who kills a parent or close relative" <This *parricide* did in everyone in his household>. *Patricide* is "the murder of one's father" or "one who kills one's father" <Oedipus was guilty of *patricide*>

partly/partially *Partly* and *partially* can be used interchangeably to mean "in some portion or part," but in that sense *partly* is the preferred choice <She's only *partly* to blame>. *Partly* has the implication of "in part, as opposed to the whole" <The rug *partly* covered the floor>, while *partially* means "incompletely, to a restricted degree" <The defender *partially* blocked the kick>. This very fine distinction is sometimes very difficult to make, as in drunkenness: *I am partly drunk* means "I'm not wholly drunk," while *I am partially drunk* means "I'm incompletely drunk," and if you can tell the difference you may have had a few yourself. When a distinction can't be made, use *partly*

pastor/rector/minister/priest/reverend *see* **reverend**

pathos/bathos *see* **bathos**

peace/piece *Peace* is "the state of harmony, tranquility, and nonaggression" <Our country may not have declared war, but we could hardly be said to be at *peace*>. A *piece* is "a portion of a whole" <I don't want just a *piece,* I want the whole pie>

peaceful/peaceable Sometimes used for each other, *peaceful* and *peaceable* have distinct senses that should be kept separate. *Peaceful* means "characterized by peace; tranquil; at ease" <We spent a *peaceful* afternoon while the kids were at Grandma's>. *Peaceable* means "inclined toward peace; promoting harmony and calm" <a *peaceable* group of activists who make their point quietly, without disrupting everyone else>

peak/pique A *peak* is "the topmost point," whether on a mountain, a hat, a sail, or in the course of developing something <I'd reached my *peak,* where I could run faster and farther than I ever had before>. *Pique* is "anger or resentment" when used as a noun, and is often employed in the phrase *fit of pique* <I felt a good deal of *pique* when she said I was unqualified for this job>. As a verb, *pique* means "to excite or arouse" <His proposal *piqued* her curiosity> or "to anger" <She was *piqued* by his flagrant sexism>

peer/pier A *peer* is "a member of British nobility" <I don't care if you're an earl, a baron, a viscount, a marquess, or a duke, you're still a *peer*> or "an equal" <He's always uncomfortable, even among his *peers*>. As a verb, *peer* means "to look closely" <She *peered* into the dimly lit room>. A *pier* is "a structure built in the water for loading and unloading ships" <Let's sit out on the *pier* and watch the tide come in>. *Peer pressure* is "the force for conformity with one's equals" <*Peer pressure* made him a straight-A student>; *pier pressure* would be "the force exerted by a dock" if it were a term anyone used

pendent/pendant *Pendent* is the more frequently used spelling for the adjective meaning "overhanging"

<The *pendent* rocks sat just above the path we took>, "dangling" <ripe, *pendent* apples slightly out of reach>, or "awaiting decision" <The case remains *pendent* after all this time>. *Pendant* is a noun that is most frequently used to mean "something hanging from something else, such as jewelry, a lamp, or a sculptured architectural ornament" <a beautiful *pendant,* filigreed gold, that hung from a leather thong around his neck>. Just to make sure everything is as confusing as it can be, however, *pendant* is an alternate spelling of *pendent,* and *pendent* is an alternate spelling of *pendant*

penguin/puffin *Penguins* and *puffins* are both aquatic birds that often sport black-and-white, tuxedolike feathers. The *penguin* is flightless and lives in the southern hemisphere, while the *puffin* can fly and prefers to remain in the northern parts of our planet <Although some argue that Opus looks more like a *puffin,* his aversion to flying makes it certain he's really a *penguin*>

penury/poverty *Penury* is "an extreme lack of money or other resources" <Our *penury* was such that we lost our house and couldn't afford food>. *Poverty,* "a lack of means" or "insufficient resources," is generally less dire <Her family spent years in *poverty,* but her mom always made sure they had something to eat>

people/peoples *People,* a singular or plural noun, refers to "human beings" generally <There sure are a lot of *people* here> or "the electorate" <The *people* overwhelmingly rejected McGovern>. *Peoples* is only used to mean "human beings with common ancestry, beliefs, geographical location, or political ties" <the *peoples* of the Pacific Basin>. When talking about such a group as a whole, *people* should be used <the African *people*> *see* **persons/people**

perceptive/insightful *see* **insightful**

peremptory/preemptive *Peremptory* has a legal sense, "stopping action, debate, or delay" <A *peremptory* motion forced the bill to a vote> and a related, more general meaning, "undeniable" <a *peremptory* conclusion based on all the available evidence>; it can also mean "urgent" <a *peremptory* call to meeting> or "arrogant" <his haughty, *peremptory* attitude>. *Preemptive* has very different meanings, including "having to do with the acquisition of land before it is made available to others," "having to do with the acquisition of something in advance" <A *preemptive* bid made the auction unnecessary>, or "self-initiated" <*preemptive* air and ground attacks on an unsuspecting foe>

perfect/prefect *see* **prefect**

perimeter/parameter *see* **parameter**

periodic/periodical Both *periodic* and *periodical* mean "occurring regularly" <Time for our *periodic* checkup> <a *periodical* get-together>. *Periodical* is also used in the same sense in reference to publications, both as an adjective <*The Sporting News* is the best *periodical* publication around when it comes to baseball> and as a noun <It's her favorite *periodical*>

perpetrate/perpetuate To *perpetrate* is "to commit or carry out" <I wouldn't want to *perpetrate* a joke like that on the American public> <*perpetrate* a crime>. The sound-alike *perpetuate* means "to cause to continue or last" <Nazis hoped to *perpetuate* their evil>

persecute/prosecute To *persecute* someone is "to harass; to annoy," especially to do so because of someone's beliefs or associates <Nixon felt the press was trying to *persecute* him>. To *prosecute* is "to bring legal action against" <No one ever *prosecuted* Nixon for his purported cover-up> or "to pursue or carry on" <The captain *prosecuted* his duties even as he stood in water up to his waist>

person/human/human being *see* **human**

personal/personnel Both terms deal with people, but that's all they have in common. *Personal* means "intimate" <Don't get *personal* with me>, "done in the presence of another" <a *personal* audience with the pope>, or "directed to or intended for a specific person" <I get to open all her mail, even the items marked "personal">. *Personnel* is "the employees of a company," whether considered as a single unit <The *personnel* isn't the problem, the machinery is> or as a group of individuals <Our *personnel* are highly competitive>; it can also be used as the name of the department within a company that deals with the employees

persons/people When talking about larger, uncounted, or indefinite groups of human beings, *people* is the word to use <A lot of these *people* would like to see the show>. *Persons* should be reserved for small, countable groups <Only four *persons* showed up on opening night>, a sense which can also be served by *people* <Six out of seven *people* I've talked to think using *persons* is an affectation> *see* **people/peoples**

perspective/prospective *Perspective* is a noun, *prospective* an adjective. They also have very different meanings.

In general, *perspective* is "a specific view," whether in drawing and painting <the use of *perspective* to give a sense of bulk>, in nature <from this *perspective,* high overlooking the river>, or as someone's personal point of view <From my *perspective* it seems this strike should have ended long ago>. *Prospective* means "likely to happen, occur, or begin being" <*prospective* parents> <a *prospective* employer>

persuade/convince *see* **convince**

peruse/browse *see* **browse**

petit/petite/petty *Petit* means "of secondary importance" and is used mostly in legal terminology <*petit* larceny>. *Petite* refers strictly to the size of a person, usually a woman; it means "of a small, slender build" <Who was that *petite* lass I saw you with?>. *Petty* has the meaning "of secondary or no importance," much like *petit;* it also can be used in the sense "small-minded" <a *petty* outlook on life>

phantasm/phantom Either *phantasm* or *phantom* can be used to mean "a ghost" or "an imaginary, visionary, or unreal thing"; *phantom* can also mean "a dreaded, inescapable thing" <the *phantom* of child abuse>

phase/faze *see* **faze**

phenomenon/phenomena *Phenomenon* is the singular form of this noun; it means "a fact or event, especially an unusual one." The plural form is *phenomena.* Make sure the verb agrees with whichever form is used <This is an interesting *phenomenon*> <*Phenomena* like out-of-body experiences and astral projection are hard to comprehend>

photocopy/copy/Xerox *see* **Xerox**

physiology/physiognomy These similar sounding words are very different in meaning. *Physiology* is "the study of bodily functions" or simply "bodily functions" <My *physiology* is such that I can't eat regular meals>. *Physiognomy* means "a person's facial features" <Pain was etched on her *physiognomy*>

pidgin/pigeon Pronunciation is all that these words have in common. *Pidgin* is "a simplified language that incorporates some parts of a local language and is used by those who do not speak each other's language" <She speaks Ga, he speaks Twi, but they both speak *pidgin* English quite well>. A *pigeon* is, of course, "a type of bird" <*pigeons* pooping on public statues>

pie/tart *see* **tart**

piece/peace *see* **peace**

pier/peer *see* **peer**

pier/wharf/dock/jetty *see* **dock**

pique/peak *see* **peak**

piteous/pitiable/pitiful In the sense "deserving or arousing pity," these words are synonymous <the *piteous* plight of the homeless>. *Pitiable* and *pitiful* are synonyms in a second sense, "arousing pity mixed with contempt" <a *pitiful* attempt at intelligent conversation>

place/locale/locality *see* **locale**

pled/pleaded Either *pled* or *pleaded* can be used as the past tense of *plead,* "to argue, implore, or make a plea" <She *pleaded* guilty to the charge> <He *pled* with her not to go>

plethora/abundance A *plethora* of something is "an excess or overabundance" of that thing <a *plethora* of tasks to achieve>. An *abundance* is "an ample amount" <an *abundance* of food and drink>. While either word describes having more than is necessary, *abundance* is used when there's a bit more than enough, and *plethora* describes having even more than that, to the point of serious excess

plurality/majority *see* **majority**

podium/lectern *see* **lectern**

politics is/politics are The word *politics,* much like the activity the word describes, is a tricky one. It can be singular or plural, depending on how it's used. In the senses "the art of governing," "activities of a political nature," or "positioning for power," it takes a singular construction <*Politics makes* strange bedfellows> <Office *politics is* something I'd rather not get involved in>. When used to mean "one's political beliefs or principles" it's constructed as a plural <Her *politics are* somewhat to the left of Karl Marx>

pore/pour *Pore* can operate as a noun meaning "a small opening in the skin of an animal or other membrane" <Clogged *pores* lead to pimples> and as a verb in the sense "to examine closely" <She *pored* over her chemistry homework>. *Pour* is used solely as a verb meaning "to shower or stream" <I *pour* my beer down the side of the glass> or "to go forth in a large flow"

<Teens *poured* out of the concert hall>. The two words are never interchangeable

port/harbor *see* **harbor**

port/starboard *Port* is "the left side of a ship or airplane." *Starboard* is "the right side of a ship or airplane." Both directions are determined by looking forward while aboard

possible/probable The difference between *possible* and *probable* is one of likelihood. That which is *possible* is "conceivable, within the realm of what can occur or be done," however unlikely it is <It's *possible* this book will sell enough copies for me to retire>. Something that's *probable* is "likely" <It's *probable* this book will eventually earn back its advance> *see* **feasible/possible, hypothetical/possible, viable/workable/possible**

practical/practicable These words are similar in meaning but are applied somewhat differently. *Practical* describes people, acts, or things that have proven "prudent, efficient, or economical" <A *practical* artist knows how to deal with the business world>. *Practicable* is used to mean "feasible, apparently workable" and generally describes plans that have not yet been tried <NASA is having a hard time finding a *practicable* solution to exploding solid-fuel booster rockets>

practically/virtually *see* **virtually**

pray/prey *Pray* is a verb meaning "to address God in prayer" or, more broadly, "to beseech" <I *pray* you, please leave us alone>. *Prey,* which can be a verb or a noun, has to do with predators and their victims: As a verb it means "to attack, devour, seize, or lay waste"

<He *preys* upon little old women>; as a noun it's "a victim" or "an animal taken for food" <Rabbits are *prey* to many carnivores>

precede/proceed To *precede* is "to go before" <Age *precedes* beauty in some circles>. To *proceed* is "to continue" or "to come forth" <Lava *proceeded* from the crack in the earth>

precedence/precedents *Precedence* means "priority" and frequently appears with the word *take* <The triage crew decides which emergencies take *precedence* over the others>. *Precedents* is a plural noun meaning "previous cases or events taken as examples" <The Supreme Court could find no *precedents* for a case like this>

precipitate/precipitous *Precipitate* has several meanings that are its alone, both as a verb meaning "to throw down," "to cause to happen abruptly," and "to cause to separate from a solution" as well as the noun sense "a substance separated from a solution." But it is as an adjective that it becomes confused with *precipitous. Precipitate,* the adjective, means "in a headlong manner, violently hurried" or "hasty, reckless" and is used to describe people and their activities <a *precipitate* dash into a burning building>. *Precipitous,* which is always an adjective, means "steep" and is mostly used to describe physical conditions <a *precipitous* climb up the steps of the Eiffel Tower>. These adjectival distinctions should not be blurred by carelessly interchanging one for the other

predominant/predominate *Predominant* is used as an adjective meaning "having the most importance or authority" <the *predominant* player of his era>. *Predominate* is mostly used as a verb in the senses "to prevail" or "to dominate" <She *predominates* the art world>. Although some dictionaries suggest that *predominate* can be used as an adjective in place of *predominant,* it's wise to reserve *predominate* for situations where a verb is called for and to use *predominant* when an adjective is needed

preemptive/peremptory *see* **peremptory**

preface/foreword *see* **foreword**

prefect/perfect A *prefect* is "a chief administrator or official" <the *prefect* of police>. *Perfect* can be an adjective meaning "without fault or omission" <A *perfect* world would have no war> or a verb meaning "to make complete or faultless" <I'll *perfect* this writing business yet>. Neither can be used for the other

pregnant/expecting/expectant *see* **expecting**

prerequisite/requirement/requisite *see* **requirement**

prescribe/proscribe To *prescribe* means "to give a rule or order" or, more commonly, "to write an order for the preparation and use of a therapeutic agent" <The doctor *prescribed* bed rest>. To *proscribe* is "to forbid or prohibit" <The doctor *proscribed* alcohol and red meat, her favorite drink and food>. The difference between the *e* and the *o* is the difference between insisting on doing something and insisting on not doing something

presently The undisputed sense of *presently* is "soon" <I'll be along *presently*>. The word is also widely used to mean "now" <No candidate is *presently* dominating the field>, but many purists consider this slang or dialect usage. To avoid the slings and arrows of picky pedants, use *now* when the meaning is "at the present time"

presume/assume Both *presume* and *assume* mean "to suppose." But *presume* is used when the supposition is not fully supported by evidence and may even be incorrect; it often implies a question or doubt <I *presume* we're invited to your party>. *Assume* also takes something for granted, but the supposition is usually an apparently safe one <I can only *assume* from your hemming and hawing that we're not invited to your party>

presumptive/presumptuous Although both words are based on *presume,* they carry a presumption to different extremes. Something described as *presumptive* is thought of as "having reasonable grounds for acceptance or belief" <It was *presumptive* of us to think there would be long lines for this film>. *Presumptuous,* on the other hand, means "impudently bold, arrogant" <It was *presumptuous* of you to think I would acquiesce to blackmail>

pretense/pretext *Pretense* is a broad term that is used to describe any of a number of actions or claims, mostly untrue ones; it can be used to mean "a claim of knowledge," "an ostentatious or unjustified act," "an insincere effort," "make-believe," "fakery," or "a pretended purpose masking one's real purpose." In this last sense it is synonymous with *pretext* <He made no *pretext* about his reason for being there; he wanted her money>. *Pretext* is also used in a related way, meaning "an excuse" <find some *pretext* to avoid being drafted>

preventive/preventative Although both words have the same meanings—"something that prevents something else" as a noun and "designed to obstruct" or "precautionary" as an adjective <*preventive* medicine>—*preventative* is frowned upon as a needlessly lengthened variant. *Preventive* is preferred for all senses

prey/pray *see* **pray**

priest/reverend/pastor/rector/minister *see* **reverend**

principle/principal *Principle,* which only serves as a noun, means "a moral rule or overarching law" <the *principle* of doing unto others what you wish done unto you>. *Principal* can be an adjective meaning "main" <The *principal* difference between you and a millionaire is your poverty> or a noun in the senses "a person in charge, especially at a school" <Mr. Wetherbee is the *principal* at Riverside High>, "the main performer" <She's the *principal* in this year's *Nutcracker*>, "money or capital lent or borrowed" <You barely start to repay the *principal* on a mortgage in the first few years>, or "the main support in a building's framing." Use *principle* whenever there are moral, religious, or legal issues involved; otherwise, the correct choice is *principal*

prior to/before *see* **before**

probable/possible *see* **possible**

proceed/precede *see* **precede/proceed**

profane/vulgar/obscene *see* **obscene**

prognosis/diagnosis *see* **diagnosis**

prone/supine Both *prone* and *supine* have to do with being in a horizontal position, but *prone* is "lying face down" while *supine* is "lying on one's back." *Prone* has the added sense of "tending to a certain trait" <*prone* to accidents>

prophecy/prophesy Both words deal with predictions of the future, often those handed to a prophet by a divine being. *Prophecy,* which ends in a long *e* sound, is the noun meaning "a prediction" <My *prophecy* for your child is health and good fortune> or "the power to foretell the future" <The gift of *prophecy* is one I do not have>. *Prophesy,* which ends with a long *i* sound, is the verb meaning "to predict or foretell through prophecy" <Not even Dean Witter can *prophesy* where the market will be in two years>

proportional/proportionate As adjectives meaning "corresponding in proportion or ratio," *proportional* and *proportionate* are synonymous <A *proportional* share of the profits go to the shareholders> <I served a *proportionate* amount of food to each guest>. *Proportional* is the word used when the sense of "in required or mandated proportions" is expressed <*proportional* representation>, and it can also be used as a noun in mathematics meaning "a constant ratio." *Proportionate* also has a unique use, as a verb meaning "to proportion"

proposal/proposition In the sense "a suggestion put forth to be considered," *proposal* and *proposition* are synonymous. But be conscious of the difference between them when talking about relations between men and women, where a *proposal* is "an offer of marriage" and a *proposition* is "a suggestion to engage in sexual intercourse"; in this latter sense *proposition* can also be used as a verb <After accepting his *proposal* she *propositioned* him>

proscribe/prescribe *see* **prescribe**

prosecute/persecute *see* **persecute**

prospective/perspective *see* **perspective**

protagonist/antagonist A *protagonist* in literature and drama is "the lead character" <I am the *protagonist* of my life story>. In other fields, the *protagonist* is "the leader or champion." An *antagonist* is "an adversary or competitor" <The batter stands at home plate glaring at his *antagonist* on the mound>. There can be only one *protagonist* in a story, making a phrase like *main protagonist* redundant; the *protagonist* may face as many *antagonists* as a storyteller wishes to provide, however

proved/proven While at one time *proven* was thought to be completely unacceptable as the past participle of *prove,* it is now considered the equal of *proved* in all cases but one <It was *proven* that calling such use of the term incorrect could not be *proved*>. The one exception to the rule is when an adjective is needed immediately before a noun, when *proven* is much more commonly used <a *proven* outfielder with a strong arm>

puffin/penguin *see* **penguin**

pulse/heartbeat A *pulse* is "the throbbing in one's arteries caused by the pumping of blood," which can be detected in many places throughout the body. A *heartbeat* is "the sound made by the contraction of one's heart," and can be heard only in the chest. Figuratively, a *heartbeat* is "a very small distance" <Dan Quayle is rumored to be only a *heartbeat* away from the presidency>, while a *pulse* is "an underlying opinion or feeling" <Marketing

experts try to keep their fingers on the *pulse* of American desires>

pupil/student In the sense "one who is being educated in school or by a tutor," *pupil* and *student* are interchangeable. Some usage experts maintain that *pupil* should be reserved for young children and *student* for older recipients of education. It's safe to use *pupil* for those up to high school age; older students should be called *students*

purposely/on purpose/purposefully All three terms operate as adverbs meaning "with purpose," but shades of meaning differentiate one from the other two of them. *Purposely* and *on purpose* mean "deliberately" or "with an express purpose" <She *purposely* left her wallet on the desk to test his honesty>. *Purposefully* means "meaningfully" or "determinedly" <Jefferson *purposefully* signed his name in large script on the Declaration of Independence>. *Purposely* and *on purpose* describe an action that's done with intention, but not necessarily one done with some underlying goal or meaning, which is what's implied by *purposefully*

purposive/purposeful In the sense "having a purpose," *purposive* and *purposeful* are synonymous <a *purposeful* exchange between American and Soviet leaders>

put (someone) on/put (someone) down *Put on* means "to mislead or string along" <Don't *put me on,* just tell me if I won or not>. To *put down* is "to denigrate or make fun of" <Don't *put her down* just because she's successful; *put her down* because she's a jerk>. Either phrase can also be used as a noun or adjective <He called me a commie and thought it was a *put-down*> <Her expertise at *put-ons* makes even her friends wonder when she's being sincere>

qualitative/quantitative *Qualitative* means "having to do with quality" <Our *qualitative* evaluation of your work shows that you make shoddy goods>. *Quantitative* means "having to do with quantity or amount" <Our *quantitative* evaluation of your work shows you are producing 375 pieces an hour>. *Qualitative* has to do with how good something is, *quantitative* with how many there are

questionable/questioning *Questionable* has to do with the quality or trustworthiness of something; it means "doubtful or dubious" <The decision to send U.S. soldiers to Vietnam was of *questionable* merit>. *Questioning* means "inquiring," with no implied distrust or misgiving <A *questioning* mind is one open to new ideas>

queue/cue A *queue* is "a braid of hair" or "a line" <You wait in the *queue* while I call Buzzy>. *Cue* has several senses, including "a braid of hair," "a word, phrase, or action that signals an actor to say or do something" <I was waiting in the wings for my *cue* but I must have dozed off>, and "a billiards stick" <You can't play eight-ball without a *cue*>. The billiards sense is never represented by the word *queue*

queue/line In Britain people generally call a group of people arranged in orderly fashion, one behind the other, a *queue,* and they wait *in* a *queue.* In the U.S. this same group of people is usually referred to as a *line,* and people wait *on* or in a *line.* Use of *line* in Britain or *queue* in the U.S. is likely to raise some eyebrows, but either is correct in either locale. And if a Briton objects to *line,* just mention that it's been used by no less an authority than Shakespeare *see* **in line/on line**

quick/quickly Both *quick* and *quickly* are used as adverbs meaning "in a speedy manner," although *quick* is sometimes frowned upon as being inferior because it lacks the *ly* ending found on most adverbs. In speech or dialogue *quick* is neat, functional, and perfectly correct <Get over here *quick*!>; it makes haste in getting the meaning across. *Quickly* is more appropriate in formal writing <She *quickly* got to the point>

quietness/quietude Both words have to do with quiet, but in different ways. *Quietness* is "a lack of noise or sound" and generally refers to external quiet <An eerie *quietness* fell over the party once the cops came>. *Quietude* is "a condition of repose or peacefulness" and refers to a lack of internal noise and confusion <the *quietude* evident on the faces of those who live a life of contemplation>.

Quietude can often be termed *quietness* but *quietness* is usually not *quietude,* it's just less noise

quoted/quoth In most everyday contexts, *quoted* is the correct word to use; it's the past tense of *quote,* "to speak or cite the words of another" <He *quoted* her confession word for word>. *Quoth,* meaning "said," is not used in modern English except when making a play on Edgar Allan Poe's famous raven <To show he meant business, when the press conference ended, *quoth* the spokesman, "There's the door">; when it is used, it should only be employed in the first or third person, and it should appear before the subject

rabbit/rabid A *rabbit* is "a small, furry mammal with long ears." *Rabid* is an adjective meaning "having rabies" <a *rabid* dog> or "furious, driven" <a *rabid* desire for a drink>

racket/racquet *Racket* can be used in the sense "a lot of noise" <Do construction workers have to make such a *racket* when they work?> or to mean "a stringed paddle used to play tennis, badminton, etc." <If you're going to take on Jimmy Connors you'd better get a decent *racket*>. *Racquet* is an alternate spelling that is used only in the meanings having to do with tennis, badminton, and so forth <I haven't picked up a *racquet* in more than ten years>. To be sure of being correct, use *racket* in all cases

rack/wrack For such noun senses as "a shelf or frame for holding things," "a medieval torture machine that stretches people," "a bar with teeth that fit into a gear," or "a triangular frame used to place balls at the start of a game of pool," the correct word is *rack.* It can also be used as a verb meaning "to torment" <The pain of her loss *racked* the dead man's mother's every waking moment> or "to torture by stretching" <He was *racked* until he thought his arms would come off>. And *rack* appears in such phrases as *rack and pinion,* "a steering mechanism used in cars," *rack (one's) brains,* "to think hard," and *rack up,* "to score points in a sport." *Wrack* appears most often in the phrase *wrack and ruin,* and means "destruction, wreckage" <The army's latest attack has brought us to *wrack* and ruin>. *Wrack* can also be spelled *rack,* although some purists object to this. One way of keeping them straight is to use *wrack* when the meaning is "wreck" and to use *rack* for any other sense

rain/reign/rein *see* **reign**

raise/raze *Raise* means "to bring up, increase, cause, collect, or put forward" <You *raise* a serious problem> <My mother *raised* me well> <You can't put up the second story of this building until we've *raised* the beams>. *Raze* applies only to construction and is opposite in meaning; it is "to tear down completely" <Once we *raze* that old tenement we can begin work on the foundation of a new office building>

rang/rung Either word was once acceptable as the past tense of *ring,* "to sound a bell, buzzer, or tone," but *rang* is fast becoming the only correct form <The phone *rang* off the hook>. Avoid using *rung*

rapt/wrapped/wrapt *Rapt* means "intent, thorough," and often appears in the phrase *rapt attention* <He hung on her every word, paying *rapt* attention through-

out her talk>. *Wrapped* is the past tense of *wrap,* "to cover or envelope" <Christmas presents *wrapped* in beautiful paper>. *Wrapt* is given by some dictionary writers as an alternate spelling of *wrapped,* but its acceptance is very limited; it is also an erroneous variant of *rapt* that occasionally finds its way into print. Avoid *wrapt* altogether

rare/unprecedented *see* **unprecedented**

ravel/unravel In a rare twist of the usual rules of English, the addition of the prefix *un* to the word *ravel* leaves the meaning unchanged. Both *ravel* and *unravel* mean "to untangle" when dealing with tangled threads or the intricacies of a mystery. *Ravel* can also mean "to entangle" <The cat hopelessly *raveled* my yarn, making it impossible for me to knit with it>. Be careful to make the intended meaning of *ravel* clear through the context in which it's used, or else use *ravel* to mean "tangle" and *unravel* for its opposite

ravish/ravage *Ravish* can mean "to rape" or "to fill with rapture and joy" <I was *ravished* by the sight of the *Mona Lisa*>. *Ravage* means "to damage, devastate, or destroy" <The troops *ravaged* the village>. *Ravish* has to do with people, *ravage* with property or places

readable/legible *Readable* describes the quality of a written work, meaning "enjoyable to read" <It may not be great literature, but it's highly *readable*>. *Legible* has to do with the ability to make out the letters and words in a piece of writing, meaning "able to be discerned" <A doctor's signature is often barely *legible*> see **illegible/unreadable**

real/really With the exception of informal speech, *real* should be used only as an adjective in the sense "genuine." The right choice for an adverb meaning "genuinely" is *really* <I'm *really* happy> <This is *really* good food>

rebellion/revolt/revolution *see* **revolution**

rebuff/repel/repulse All three words have to do with turning back or refusing someone or something, but they are used somewhat differently. To *rebuff* means "to snub" and is employed in situations where a person or an action is considered inferior <Every attempt we made to get into Studio 54 was *rebuffed*>. To *repel* means "to drive back by force" <The Marines were ordered to *repel* any foreigners trying to gain entrance to the compound> or "to be pushed away or turned back because of disgust" <Before he even uttered a word, his appearance *repelled* her>. To *repulse* is "to firmly and discourteously turn away" <He thought he was hot stuff until she *repulsed* his advances> or "to cause to recoil" <The bloody horror of the accident *repulsed* him>. *Repel* and *repulse* both have the implication of disgust, but *repulse* is considered the stronger of the two

rebut/refute Both *rebut* and *refute* mean "to argue against or contradict," but they imply different results. To *rebut* is "to present the opposing view," especially in a courtroom or other legal venue <Our witnesses will *rebut* the image of the defendant presented by the prosecutor>. To *refute* means "to prove false" <Columbus *refuted* the argument that the world is flat>

receipt/recipe These words stem from a common root meaning "to receive," but they've grown far enough apart that they should not be used interchangeably in formal writing. A *receipt* is "an acknowledgment for goods, services, or money" <We can't reimburse you unless you provide a *receipt* for the taxi fare> or "an act of receiving" <on *receipt* of this notice>. A *recipe* is "a formula or directions for preparing a specific food dish" <I must have the *recipe* for this pie> or, more broadly, "a formula for achieving something" <Your plan is a *recipe* for disaster>. In the past, and currently in some parts of the U.S., *receipt* can be used to mean *recipe,* but this usage is not sufficiently widespread to be considered acceptable in most writing

reciprocal/mutual Although sometimes used interchangeably in informal contexts, these words describe different types of relations that can exist between two parties. A *reciprocal* relationship is one in which something is "done by the first party in return for something done by the second" <She wanted to make a *reciprocal* gesture, but how could she scratch his back if he wouldn't scratch hers?>. *Mutual* describes something "done or felt by each to or for the other," generally because of shared feelings and not because of an expected payback <*Mutual* respect is the cornerstone of a marriage>. *Mutual* is also used in the sense "common or joint" <our *mutual* friend> *see* **mutual/common**

re-collect/recollect Sometimes a hyphen makes all the difference. *Re-collect* means "to collect again" <He neatly stacked the magazines, then *re-collected* them after they were strewn about the house>. To *recollect* is "to remember or recall" <I *recollect* your birthday as being on the fourth>

recollect/recall Both *recollect* and *recall* mean "to remember" and imply an active search of one's memory, as opposed to something remembered without effort

recourse/resort *Recourse* and *resort* can be used interchangeably to mean "a source of help; an expedient" <We have no *recourse* but to bring in the big guns> <Ignoring the problem would be our last *resort*>. The examples show the most common constructions in which these words appear: *no recourse* and *last resort*

rector/minister/priest/reverend/pastor *see* **reverend**

recurrence/reoccurrence A *recurrence* is "a repeated happening" <A *recurrence* of skirmishes between Israeli settlers and Palestinians is inevitable>. A *reoccurrence* is "an instance of repetition" <A *reoccurrence* of these symptoms indicates a serious health problem>. *Recurrence* is used for events that happen repeatedly, while *reoccurrence,* which is a less frequently used word, is used for events that happen once again; the phrase *repeated recurrence* is redundant, but *repeated reoccurrence* is not

reduce/minimize *see* **minimize**

reevaluate/revaluate *see* **revaluate**

refer/allude *see* **allude**

regardless/irregardless *see* **irregardless**

registered/enrolled Both *registered* and *enrolled* mean "officially enlisted or signed up" <She *registered* for classes> <He *enrolled* in a correspondence school>. *Reg-*

istered is used with *for,* while *enrolled* is used with *in,* but they are otherwise interchangeable

regretful/regrettable These two have to do with feelings of regret, but differ in what is the object of that regret. *Regretful* means "feeling sorrow because of circumstances beyond one's control" and is used to describe a person <How can you not be *regretful* about the closing of your favorite restaurant?>. *Regrettable* has to do with something—an event or circumstance—that provokes regret, with the sense "causing or deserving regret" <Throwing up on the president was certainly *regrettable*>

reign/rein/rain A *reign* is "a king's or queen's period of rule" <during the *reign* of Henry VIII>; it can also be used in the sense "a predominance or influence by something" <We must endure this *reign* of terrorism> and as a verb in either of these senses. *Rein* can be used to mean "a strap that controls a horse" or more broadly "a controlling, guiding, or restraining influence"; it is usually used in the plural <The president doesn't hold the *reins* of government alone> and can also be a verb in either sense. *Rain* is "liquid precipitation" <The *rain* in Spain stays mainly in the plain>, and it, too, can be a verb <It *rains* all the time>

relation/relative In the sense of "kin," *relation* and *relative* are synonyms, and both should be used with *of* when this meaning is intended <He's no *relation* of mine> <She's a *relative* of my husband>. When used with *to,* these words mean "something that corresponds or contrasts" <Those events have little meaning in *relation* to our current circumstances> <*Relative* to yesterday's game, today's is a bore>

reluctant/reticent *Reluctant* means "unwilling, opposed" <We were *reluctant* to continue>, although it is usually employed in situations in which that unwillingness is overcome. *Reticent* can also mean "unwilling" but is mostly used in milder senses like "reserved" or "restrained" <He was *reticent* when confronted by strangers>

reparable/repairable Both *reparable* and *repairable* mean "able to be repaired or fixed." *Reparable* is usually used with regard to relations between people and appears most often in the negative *irreparable* <I'd hate to see an *irreparable* rift grow between us>. *Repairable* is usually employed in more literal applications <A broken chair is often *repairable* with only some wood glue>. Although these distinctions are often observed, either word is correct for either application

repeat/reiterate Both *repeat* and *reiterate* mean "to say or do again," but while *repeat* is used for a single instance of restating or redoing <She *repeated* her question>, *reiterate* can be used to mean "to say or do again and again, often to the point of tedium" <He *reiterated* the same tired suggestion in front of each audience he faced>

repel/repulse/rebuff *see* **rebuff**

repertoire/repertory *Repertoire* means "the songs, plays, operas, etc., a performer or company knows and is prepared to perform" <Our *repertoire* runs from Ionesco to Shakespeare> or "the range of skills or things possessed by a given person" <a limited *repertoire* of winter footwear>. *Repertory* can be used in the same senses, but has the added meanings of "a group of plays, operas, etc., performed alternately during a single season at a single theater" <presenting *The Wild Duck* and *Into the Woods* in *repertory*> or "a storehouse" <If it's not on the shelf I'll take a look in the *repertory*>

replete/complete *Replete* means "having great abundance" <a great story *replete* with juicy gossip> or "overfilled or stuffed" <I am *replete* with turkey after Thanksgiving dinner>. It should never be used in place of *complete,* which has the senses "finished" <a scrap of a novel that isn't really *complete*>, "whole and entire" <I can't believe you ate the *complete* turkey>, or "perfect" <A touch of brandy will make this evening *complete*>

repulse/rebuff/repel *see* **rebuff**

requirement/requisite/prerequisite *Requirement,* a noun, means "something necessary or desired" <Beauty is not a *requirement* for this job>. *Requisite* is more absolute, meaning "something necessary" when it's a noun or "necessary" as an adjective, with no regard for its desirability <The *requisite* training for this job includes a three-year apprenticeship>. A *prerequisite* is "something necessary for something else" and is used with the preposition *for* <The *prerequisite* for this course is a perfect score on the SATs>; it can also be used as an adjective with the preposition *to* <Completion of high school is generally *prerequisite* to college admission>. A *prerequisite* is a *requisite* of a specific type, and a *requirement* can be a *requisite* although it often is less ironclad

rescind/revoke *Rescind* and *revoke* are synonyms that mean "to take back or cancel." *Rescind* usually applies to stipulations that were previously made <Will you *rescind* that order?>, and *revoke* is used with regard to privileges that were previously granted <My license has been *revoked*>

residue/residual *Residue* is a noun meaning "what is left over, the remainder" <We found a few personal effects in the fire's *residue*>. *Residual* is usually used as an adjective meaning "leftover" <The *residual* effects of this drug are puffiness and red eyes>, although it also forms a noun with the same meaning as *residue* and can be a plural noun meaning "payments made to actors or writers for subsequent showings of a TV show or movie" <Few actors can afford to live on *residuals* alone>

resin/rosin *Resin* is "a clear or translucent substance used in varnishes, printing ink, plastics, and other products." One type of *resin* is *rosin,* which is "a translucent resin used to treat violin bows, and to make varnish, soap, and other products." Both *resin* and *rosin* can be used as verbs meaning "to treat with resin (or rosin)"

resort/recourse *see* **recourse**

responsible/accountable/liable *see* **accountable**

resume/curriculum vitae *Resume* and *curriculum vitae* are used interchangeably to mean "a summary of one's past educational and work experience." *Resume,* which can be styled with no accents, one accent over the final *e,* or accents over both *e*s, is more common and less pretentious for most contexts. In academia, however, *curriculum vitae* (also called *vitae* or *cv*) is generally considered correct

revaluate/reevaluate Both words mean "to assess the value again," but they are used in very different contexts. *Revaluate* applies exclusively to monetary value and is mostly used in discussing an increase in the value of a given currency <The Mexican government is under serious pressure to *revaluate* the peso>. *Reevaluate* is a much broader term that applies to a reassessment of something's worth in financial, personal, or social terms <It's time to *reevaluate* our relationship in light of your constant philandering>

revenge/avenge *see* **avenge**

reverend/pastor/rector/minister/priest All these words are used in reference to members of Christian clergy or Christians who officiate in religious services, but they apply differently depending on the person's job within the church and which denomination or religion is involved. *Reverend* is used mostly as an adjective, preceded by *the,* meaning "member of the clergy" <the *Reverend* Timothy Titmouse>; some Protestant denominations, such as Baptists and Methodists, use *reverend* as a noun <I'm going to visit the *reverend*> and as a form of address <We wondered if *Reverend* Titmouse was available>. *Pastor* is a noun meaning "religious leader of a congregation" in all Christian churches <The pope is the *pastor* of the Catholic Church>; it can also be used as a form of address <I didn't know you were a baseball fan, Pastor>. A *rector* is "a member of the clergy in charge of a parish," which means one who is chief administrator of a given church or district as opposed to a spiritual leader <The *rector* is worried about where we'll get funds for the church's new roof>. A *minister* is "one who performs religious functions in a church" or "a member of the clergy"; a *minister* isn't necessarily in charge of either a congregation or a parish <Members of the laity can be *ministers* in many Catholic and Protestant churches>. A *priest* is "a Roman Catholic, Anglican, Armenian, or Eastern Orthodox member of the clergy authorized to perform sacred rites of the religion" who ranks above a deacon and below a bishop in each church's hierarchy <If you need absolution, talk to a *priest*>

revive/resuscitate Both *revive* and *resuscitate* mean "to bring back to life" or "to return to consciousness"; they can be used interchangeably in a literal sense <The medical team worked frantically to *revive* her> or a figurative one <I'm not sure this organization is worth *resuscitating*>

revolution/rebellion/revolt A *revolution* is "a complete change in type of government or other system or organization" <Yippies hoped for a *revolution* that would eliminate capitalism as a driving force in America>. A *rebellion* is "an armed attempt at overthrowing a government," and generally refers to an attempt that doesn't succeed <The *rebellion* would have spread to other parts of the country if the king's guards hadn't stopped it>. A *revolt* is "an act of defiance or rebellion" that often involves armed opposition <A *revolt* in the ranks of uniformed police involved a refusal to write tickets or arrest agitators>

revolve/rotate *Revolve* can mean either "to move in an orbit around something" <The earth *revolves* around the sun> or "to spin or turn on an axis" <She could make her top *revolve* for more than two minutes on a single spin>. In its second sense, *revolve* is a synonym for *rotate* <The earth *rotates* fully once every day>.

rifle/riffle When used as verbs, *rifle* means "to ransack or plunder" <*rifle* a safe>, and *riffle* means "to thumb through, shuffle, or flip" <She *riffled* through the files looking for the deed>

right/rite/wright/write *Right* means "correct, true" <Your answer is *right*> or "in a direction opposite left" <turn *right*>; it can also mean "politically conservative" <She leans to the *right* on foreign policy issues>. A *rite* is "a ritual or religious ceremony" <a *rite* of passage for young men>. *Wright* is a combining word meaning "one who works on a given thing" <ship*wright,* play*wright*>. *Write* means "to set down letters and words" <It's sometimes easier to *write* what you mean than it is to say it>. Despite the fact that all four words sound identical, each is used only for its own specific meanings

rightist/right wing *Rightist* and *right wing* are both nouns that have to do with conservative social or political beliefs. *Rightist* applies to individuals, meaning "one who advocates or adheres to conservative principles" <Reagan has made it acceptable to be a *rightist* again>. *Right wing* applies to a group of people; it means "the faction of a political party or similar group that advocates more conservative positions" <The *right wing* of the Republican party has pushed more moderate elements out of power>

ripple/undulate *see* **undulate**

rise/arise *Rise* and *arise* can be used interchangeably to mean "to awake and leave one's bed" <I don't know why you have such trouble *rising* in the morning. When I *arise* I'm fresh as a daisy and raring to go> or "to get up or stand up" <*Rise* when the minister indicates you should><Get up off your knees, *arise* and greet the king>. *Rise* is the word that means "to increase in volume or size," whether talking about dough or a river <Allow the mixture to *rise* in a warm place overnight>. *Arise* is the right choice for the sense "to come up or be brought to the fore" <Problems *arise* all the time in this sort of work>

rise/raise *Rise* is the verb used to mean "to increase" in sentences where the verb follows the subject <Will my take-home pay *rise* next year?>, although *raise* is used as a verb in this sense when the subject comes after the verb <*Raise* my salary and I'll work even harder>. The noun form is *raise* <I hope the boss gives me a *raise*>

river/kill/stream/creek/brook *see* **kill**

road/street/avenue All three words could be defined as "a public thoroughfare," but they differ in the nature of the thoroughfare or its location. A *road* is "an open way outside urban areas." A *street* is "an urban thoroughfare" <What *road?* He ain't walking on no *road.* He's in the city now, walking on a *street*>. And an *avenue* is "a broad street."

robbery/burglary/larceny/theft *see* **burglary**

rococo/baroque *see* **baroque**

role/roll A *role* is "a character performed by an actor" <He gets so into his *role* he can't stop when the curtain comes down> or "a function" <Her *role* is to act tough when one of these wiseguys comes in>. A *roll* can be "a baked good often used to make sandwiches" <hot dog on a *roll*>, "an act of tumbling" <The gym teacher made us practice forward *rolls* all morning>, "a written document or list" <Of course I marked you absent. You

didn't answer when I called the *roll*>, or "a rapid beating on a drum" <the *rolls* and flourishes of the fife-and-drum corps>, among others. Unless the sense of "a part"—whether played by an actor or assumed by a person—is meant, the right choice is *roll*

rosin/resin *see* **resin**

round/around As an adverb or preposition meaning "in every direction," "in a circle," or "along a circular route," *round* can be used interchangeably with *around* <There were wild beasts all *round* us> <The settlers drew their wagons *around*> <Walk *round* the bend, you can't miss it>. *Round* doesn't take an apostrophe when used for *around*

rout/route/root A *rout* (pronounced ROWT) is "a lopsided defeat" <The Battle of the Little Bighorn was decidedly a *rout*> or "a swift and confused retreat" <With most of their comrades killed or wounded, they took off in a *rout*>, both senses having to do with the chaos that comes from defeat. A *route* (pronounced ROOT or ROWT) is "a specific path of travel from one place to another" <You can take any of four *routes* into the city and each is as likely to be jammed with traffic as the others>. And a *root* is "the sustenance-seeking base of a plant that holds it in place," "the embedded part of a tooth, nerve, or hair" <blond hair with black *roots*>, "the origins or antecedents of something" <Alex Haley went looking for his family's *roots*>, and "a basic part or core" <Money is the *root* of all evil>

rubble/ruble *Rubble* means "crumbled rock" or "destroyed things" <The *rubble* from the renovated apartment was piled on the curb>; in either sense it suggests a mass of useless stuff. A *ruble,* on the other hand, is anything but useless: It's "a unit of currency in the USSR"

ruff/rough A *ruff* is "a large, circular, frilly collar worn in Europe in the late sixteenth and early seventeenth centuries," "a collarlike ring of feathers or fur on an animal," or "a specific perch or sandpiper"; it also is used as a verb meaning "to take a trick with a trump" or a noun meaning "a trumping." All the senses covered by *ruff* are relatively obscure or specialized. The more common word *rough* means "not smooth" either literally <the *rough* texture of unfinished wood> or figuratively <a *rough* day>, and is also used to mean "unfinished" <a *rough* sketch>, "uneven or rugged ground or terrain" in both golf <He sliced the ball into the *rough*> and camping or hiking <She liked to get off the beaten path and into the *rough*>

rung/rang *see* **rang**

Russia/U.S.S.R. Although *Russia* is frequently used as the name of the communist nation whose capital is Moscow, this is technically incorrect. The country's true name (in English) is the Union of Soviet Socialist Republics, or more simply, the *U.S.S.R. Russia* is a shortened name of one of those republics, the Russian Soviet Federated Socialist Republic; it's also the former name of the country and was in use until the Russian Revolution of 1917. But it is no more correct to call the *U.S.S.R.* "Russia" than it is to call the U.S.A. "the colonies."

S

sac/sack A *sac* is "a pouch in or on an animal or plant," often one that holds a liquid <The scrotum is a testicular *sac*>; it is also used in baseball terminology to mean "a sacrifice." *Sack* is the more general term, meaning "a bag or pouch" <Put the groceries in the *sack*>, "a loose-fitting dress" <Not even Cinderella would be caught wearing that *sack*>, "a bed" <Let's hit the *sack*>; in baseball it means "a base" <How could I be out when he never touched the *sack?*>, and in football it means "to tackle the quarterback behind the line of scrimmage" <Sims was *sacked* five times last Sunday>

sail/sale A *sail* is "a cloth or fabric that catches the wind and propels a boat" <Raise the *sail* and get under way>; it can also be used as a verb <Let's *sail* to the Caribbean>. A *sale* is "the selling of something" <After three days on the job she made a *sale*> or "the selling of something at a discount" <The store is having a *sale* on cameras>. These words can never be used interchangeably

sank/sunk The preferred form for the past tense of *sink,* "to slip beneath water," is *sank* <Our boat *sank* only ten feet from shore>, although *sunk* is not wrong in this usage <We *sunk* far out at sea>. The past participle of *sink* is *sunk;* this means it is used in conjunction with another verb in the passive voice <The ship was *sunk*> or with another verb in the perfect tenses in the active voice <We will be *sunk* by morning>

sardonic/sarcastic/laconic *Sardonic* and *sarcastic* both have to do with making fun of someone or something, but with different shades of meaning. Something described as *sardonic* is "mocking, derisive, or cynical"; the word applies both to what is said and the accompanying facial or body expression <"I think he'd make a great world leader," she said *sardonically*>. *Sarcastic* means "expressing ridicule or openly taunting," usually with absurd contradictions or statements that don't pertain to the subject at hand; it generally applies just to what is said or the accompanying tone of voice <His *sarcastic* remarks about the "appropriateness" of her blue jeans at a formal dinner were more than she could take>. And *laconic,* which is often confused with *sardonic,* means simply "concise; using the fewest possible words"

satiate/fill In terms of hunger, both *satiate* and *fill* can mean "to satisfy an appetite," but *satiate* is usually used to mean "to oversatisfy an appetite; to feed to excess" and implies a feeling of revulsion at the thought of having more <I'm usually *full* after dinner, but after that Christmas dinner I was *satiated*>

saving/savings Advertisers, who frequently break the rules of usage for reasons only they could explain, have taken to using the phrase *a savings* <This limited offer represents a *savings* of ten dollars>. Although *ten dollars* is plural, the offer represents a single *saving.* Use *saving,* preceded by *a,* for all singular senses; reserve *savings* for those cases where more than one saving is taking place, and use it without the word *a* <This offer provides *savings* of ten dollars a month for the whole year>

say/state *see* **state**

scintilla/iota These words are synonyms meaning "an infinitesimal quantity, minute amount, or trace" <You haven't a *scintilla* of evidence> <There's hardly an *iota* of truth in that statement>

scold/chide *see* **chide**

scream/screech/shriek All three words mean "to make a loud, piercing sound," although the implied nature of that sound is different depending on which word is chosen. *Scream* connotes sudden, long sounds made because of pain, fear, or surprise; *screaming* can involve comprehensible words <"Get out of my house!" he *screamed* at the intruder>. To *screech* is to make a high-pitched, shrill, and rasping sound <She *screeched* at her class, her words sounding like nails on a blackboard>. To *shriek* means to make a very high-pitched sound, usually one that is inarticulate or that demonstrates a loss of control <After being told of her death, he *shrieked* and moaned and carried on for quite some time>. These words are usually used with regard to expressions of horror or fear, but they can also be applied to laughter. They can function as nouns in addition to the verb senses described here

scull/skull A *scull* is "an oar" or "a racing rowboat." It should never be confused with a *skull,* "the bones of the head"

sculpture/sculpt *Sculpture* and *sculpt* are interchangeable verbs meaning "to create a three-dimensional figure or model of clay, marble, wood, or metal"; they are equally acceptable in this sense. The corresponding noun is *sculpture*

sea/ocean Both *sea* and *ocean* can be used to mean "the body of saltwater covering the earth," usually preceded by the word *the* <I set forth upon the *sea*> <sail round the world upon the *ocean*>. A *sea* can also be "a large body of salt or fresh water partially or fully enclosed by land"; in this sense it is usually part of a proper name <the Mediterranean *Sea*> <the Caspian *Sea*>. An *ocean* can be "one of the four subdivisions of the salt water covering the earth" <The world's four *oceans* are the Atlantic, the Pacific, the Indian, and the Arctic> *see* bay/gulf/sound

seam/seem A *seam* can be "a line where two pieces of cloth or leather are joined" <He got so fat, he stretched his shirt's *seams* to the breaking point>. Several other lines where different parts or pieces come together are also called *seams,* including "the space between adjacent planks on a ship," "a layer of mineral, coal, or stone that lies between strata of other rock," "a scar," or "a wrinkle." *Seam* also serves as a verb meaning "to join with or as if with a seam" or "to affix lines that look like seams." *Seem* acts only as a verb and only in the sense "appear or look" <It doesn't *seem* like we'll be able to go out today>

seasonable/seasonal Both words are used as adjectives that describe things in terms of the seasons, but they do so somewhat differently. *Seasonable* means "appropriate to the season" <*Seasonable* weather in New York means a foot of snow in January and blazing heat in July> <Let's do something *seasonable* like have a picnic>. *Seasonal* means "controlled by or having to do with the season of the year," and usually applies to things that occur cyclically <A *seasonal* adjustment in employment figures takes into account the fact that there are usually more workers employed at this time of year>

secondly/second Many take it as a given that all adverbs end in *ly* and that *secondly* is therefore the only correct word meaning "in the second position or place." *Secondly* and *second* are both right in this sense. *Second* is usually the better choice when listing or enumerating items, however, because such a list should always be internally consistent and *firstly,* which is consistent with *secondly,* sounds ridiculous <I want you to hire me because, first, I'm perfectly suited to it, and *second,* I need a job> <She wanted to leave because, firstly, it was late, and *secondly,* they had a long way to go> *see* **firstly/first**

semi-/bi- *see* **bi-**

sense/sensibility *Sense,* in the meaning that's confused with *sensibility,* is "judgment, intelligence, mental capability" <The girl has no *sense;* she seems to think there will be no repercussions to unprotected sex>. *Sensi-*

bility refers to "susceptibility, sensitivity, the ability to feel things" and is often used in the plural <His *sensibilities* were offended by the existence of such poverty in the midst of so much wealth>. *Sense* has to do with the rational mind, *sensibility* with the emotions

sensitive/sensitize *Sensitive* is the adjective form meaning "responsive to or affected by outside stimulation" <He's very *sensitive* to criticism> <She's *sensitive* to dairy products>. *Sensitize,* a verb, means "to make sensitive" <I was *sensitized* to the needs of others>

sensual/sensuous/sexual All three adjectives have been applied in recent years to the gratification of the senses obtained from having sex. There are differences between them regarding the nature of that gratification that are useful to the careful writer. *Sensual* means "having to do with satisfaction of physical desire and fleshly appetites" <Her lust was quenched by three days of nonstop *sensual* enjoyment>. *Sensuous* has the sense of "having to do with the satisfaction of the esthetic senses" <The *sensuous* man is one who gets as much, if not more, satisfaction from looking at a beautiful woman as he does from making love to her>. *Sexual* means "having to do with sex," without the implied pleasure inherent in *sensual* or *sensuous* <He was just one more in a seemingly endless series of *sexual* liaisons>

serpent/snake *Serpent* and *snake* are interchangeable, both meaning "a scaly reptile with a long, tapered body"

set/sit Most of the time, *set* is the correct choice if a transitive verb (one requiring a direct object) is needed <He *set* the table> <*Set* that gun down nice and slow>, and *sit* is used if an intransitive verb (one without a direct object) is employed <Feel free to *sit* down if you're tired>. Unfortunately, this is not an ironclad rule, so there are numerous exceptions: <The sun *set* behind the mountains> <That jacket *sets* (or *sits)* so perfectly on you> <The hen *set* (or *sat)* on her clutch of eggs> <I'll *sit* myself down and think this over>. If a usage decision is being made on guesswork, follow the rule regarding direct objects; otherwise check a dictionary to see if that specific situation is given as an example

sex/gender *see* **gender**

shade/shadow In the sense "shelter from the light and heat of the sun," *shade* and *shadow* are interchangeable <In Ghana, only idiots and white people leave the *shade* at midday> <Let's sit in the *shadow* of that chestnut tree>. There are also a number of meanings that are exclusive to one or the other of these words. A *shade* can also be "a ghost or spirit," "a cover that obscures part of a lamp's light," or "a window covering." *Shadow* has the added senses of "a body-shaped patch of shade made made by blocking the sun with that body," "a constant companion" <I'd like you to meet Bert and his *shadow,* Trixie the dog>, "a small amount" <without a *shadow* of doubt>, or "a pall" <Her departure cast a *shadow* on the meeting>

shall/will Simply put, *shall* is dead; it is not used in American English in the late twentieth century, even in formal, serious writing, and it comes across as affected and snobbish. The "rule," which was never very widely applied, states that *shall* is used to express future tense in the first person <I *shall* come to your house tomorrow> and to express determination, obligation, inevitability, and requirement in the second and third persons <You *shall* not set foot in this house again>. *Shall* was also supposed to be used in all persons to show an indefinite future tense in conditional clauses <If you *shall* ever need me, I am but a heartbeat away>. But current usage allows the use of *will* in any of these circumstances

shanty/chantey A *shanty* is "a small shack" <On the outskirts of the opulent city is a village consisting of hundreds of *shanties*>. A *chantey* (which can also be spelled *chanty, shantey,* or *shanty*) is "a work song sung by sailors" <Popeye likes nothing better than to sing a *chantey* while swabbing the poop deck>. For those who like mnemonics, remember *shanty* is a *sh*ack and *chantey* is a *ch*ant

shear/sheer *Shear* is mostly used as a verb meaning "to cut, shave, strip away, or break" <Superman could *shear* the rocks off that cliff with his bare hands>. As a noun, it is used to mean "stress caused by the action of differing pressures" <Wind *shear* can bring an airplane to the ground much faster than intended> or, in the plural *shears,* "a cutting device similar to a very large scissors" <Springtime is when we put the *shears* to the sheep>. *Sheer* is most often an adjective meaning "pure" <She landed in the hospital through *sheer* bad luck>, "steep" <Once past the base camp, you ascend a *sheer* rock face to reach the peak>, or "translucent" <The *sheer* material of his shirt exposed his magnificent pecs>. *Sheer* is also used occasionally as a verb in the sense "to swerve" <The racer had to *sheer* off the straightaway to avoid a pedestrian>

ship/boat *see* boat

shoot/chute *Shoot* is most often used as a verb in a wide variety of senses that mostly have to do with propulsion of one kind or another. It can mean "to fire a gun," "to hit with something fired from a gun" <Did you *shoot* him?>, "to send out or move rapidly" <Rickey *shoots* out of the batter's box so quickly he can almost beat the batted ball to first base>, "to propel a ball or puck at a goal in soccer, basketball, hockey, etc.," "to slide" <*Shoot* some copies across the table, please> <*shoot* a bolt>, "to film or photograph," and "to grow out or up" <The bulb *shoots* its new stem skyward>. It can also be used to mean "go ahead and talk" <I'm all ears. *Shoot*>, and appears in such familiar phrases as *shoot [one's] mouth off, shoot for [something], shoot down, shoot up, shoot the rapids,* and *shoot the works. Chute* is nowhere near so diverse in its meanings; they are "an inclined trough or slide" <He took the boxes from the truck and placed them on the *chute*> <a coal *chute*>, "a sudden, downward incline," especially in a river <She could barely keep her canoe upright going through the last *chute,* and that was an easy one>, and "a parachute" when it serves as a noun, or "to move on, with, or as though on a chute" when it's a verb

shortsighted/nearsighted *see* **nearsighted**

should/would The basic differentiation between these words is that *should* has to do with what needs to be done, while *would* deals with what is desired. *Should* acts as a part of a verb that implies an imperative <You *should* go to school if you hope to graduate>, an expectation <He *should* be here before supper if the trains are running on schedule>, or a possibility <If I *should* fall in love again, it won't be with someone like her>. *Would* also acts as a part of a verb, similar to *will* but with the sense of a condition <You *would* like it if you tried it>, an expectation <She *would* go and drink up all the beer before we get back>, a periodic event <Self-help books *would* appear whenever times got tough>, or probability <I *would* be an old man before the Cubs won the pennant>; it's also used to be polite in asking a question <*Would* you please take a seat?> or making a statement <I *would* think it's not the sort of thing one should do here>

shriek/scream/screech *see* **scream**

sic *Sic* means "thus" and is used to indicate that what preceded it is supposed to be that way, even if it seems odd or is misspelled. It's mostly used when quoting other written material to let readers and typesetters know that even if the word or phrase is incorrect it should remain as is. *Sic* is placed in brackets or parentheses and should be italicized or underlined <According to one source, "She praid *[sic]* for rain every day">

sight/site/cite *see* **cite**

signal/single/singular *Signal,* as an adjective, means "unusual, especially unusually good or unusually bad" <Pitching a no-hitter is a *signal* accomplishment>. *Single,* or more frequently *singular,* can be used to mean "individual, unique, exceptional" <DiMaggio's consecutive-game hitting streak is a *singular* (or *single)* event in baseball history>. *Signal* is used for events or people that aren't encountered every day; *singular* or *single* are appropriate for things that aren't likely to ever happen again

simian/ape/monkey *Simian* is the general term meaning "an ape or monkey." An *ape* is "a large, tailless primate," such as a chimpanzee, a gorilla, or an orangutan; *ape* can also be used generally to mean "a primate." A *monkey* is "a small, long-tailed primate," although it too can mean "a primate." If a specific primate is referred to, use *ape* or *monkey* as appropriate; if the type of primate is unspecified, it should properly be called a *simian*

since/because *see* **because**

site/sight/cite *see* **cite**

skillet/griddle *see* **griddle**

skull/scull *see* **scull**

slake/slack *Slake* is most often used to mean "to quench" <A tall glass of water is the best way to *slake* your thirst>; it can also mean "to moderate" <Appeals for unity did little to *slake* the crowd's anger> or "to chemically combine lime and water." *Slack* can also be used in the sense "to chemically combine lime and water," although it is more frequently used to mean "to loosen" <*Slack* that line a little so it will reach over here> or "to evade or be lazy about work," often in the phrase *slack off* <If you spent less time thinking up ways to *slack* off you'd be able to get your work done in half the time>

slander/libel *see* **libel**

sled/sleigh Both *sled* and *sleigh* mean "a vehicle with runners used for travel on snow or ice," but a *sled* is usually a small vehicle of this type used by children on hills, while a *sleigh* is the larger, horse-drawn vehicle used to transport people and goods <The kids want to bring

their *sled* to the park today> <dashing through the snow in a one-horse open *sleigh*>

sludge/slush *Sludge* and *slush* are both nasty, wet substances, but they are somewhat different substances. *Sludge* is "mud" or "a mudlike substance" <When the river overflows its banks, we get *sludge* from the sewage treatment plant in our yard>. *Slush* is usually "partly melted snow" <Winter storms are pretty, but the next day the sidewalks are covered with *slush*>, although it can also mean "soft mud," "paper pulp suspended in water," or "used cooking grease." To avoid confusion, use *sludge* for mud and similar gunk and *slush* for melted snow

slum/ghetto *see* **ghetto**

small/marginal/minimal *see* **marginal**

smell/stink/odor *see* **odor**

snake/serpent *see* **serpent**

social/sociable *Social* and *sociable* are interchangeable in the senses "friendly, inclined to enjoy the company of others" <He's a real hermit, not *sociable* at all> and "marked by friendliness or enjoyable interaction" <It turned out to be a very *social* evening after all>. *Social* is the word to choose for meanings such as "designed for companionship" <a *social* club> or "having to do with human interaction" <She's a great speechmaker but not very good at the *social* amenities>

sofa/couch *see* **couch**

solicitor/barrister/attorney/lawyer *see* **barrister**

soluble/solvable Either *soluble* or *solvable* can be used to mean "capable of being solved" <It's a *soluble* issue but one better taken up by the committee as a whole> <I'm sure this week's crossword is *solvable,* but I can't figure it out>. *Soluble* also has the meaning "capable of being dissolved or emulsified in a liquid" <Oil is not *soluble* in water>

some time/sometime *Some time* is a phrase meaning "an unspecified amount of time" <I hope to make *some time* available for my family when this book is finished>. *Sometime* is an adverb meaning "at some time" <We hope to get there *sometime* today>; it is also used as an adjective meaning "former" <Jimmy Carter is a *sometime* president>. *Sometime* is also used as an adjective meaning "occasional" <a writer, researcher, and *sometime* lecturer>, although this sense is frowned on by many usage experts and is best avoided in formal writing

sort of/kind of *Sort of* and *kind of* can be interchanged for the meaning "type of" <I hate this *sort of* job> <She likes this *kind of* music>. Many speakers and quite a few writers insert the words *a* or *an* after *sort of* or *kind of* <I hate this *sort of a* job>, but these articles add nothing to the meaning of the sentence and serve only to clutter it up; they are better left out

sound/bay/gulf *see* **bay**

spatial/spacious *Spatial* means "having to do with or existing in space" <The *spatial* characteristics of Carnegie Hall were not very much affected by the recent remodeling>; the word has no connotation about the size of a given space. *Spacious,* on the other hand, does deal with size; it means "large" <A *spacious* two-bedroom apartment would make our lives a lot easier>

special/especial *see* **especial**

specially/especially *see* **especially**

special/unique/unusual *see* **unique**

species/genus *see* **genus**

sprang/sprung As the past tense of *spring,* "to leap, jump, rise up, or shoot," *sprang* and *sprung* are both acceptable <He *sprang* from his bed to see what was the matter> <She *sprung* forth from behind the curtains, scaring everyone to death>. *Sprung* also serves as the past participle of *spring* <In a death-defying stunt, they were *sprung* from two cannons>

sprain/strain In discussing bodily injury, there is little practical difference between these two. The only variance is that a *sprain* is usually the result of a sudden, violent wrenching of muscles or ligaments <I *sprained* my ankle trying to make that turn>, while a *strain* of muscles or ligaments is caused by using them either for too long or to do too much <Carrying a forty-pound pack twenty-five miles *strained* my legs and my back>

stalactite/stalagmite Both words name mineral formations found in caves. A *stalactite* is "a conical mineral formation attached to a cave's ceiling," and a *stalagmite* is "a conical mineral formation standing on a cave's floor." The rocky problem of remembering which is which can be solved by learning this simple saying: A *stalactite* holds on *tight,* a *stalagmite* pushes up with all its *might*

stanch/staunch These words have been so confused with each other that each is now accepted as a variant spelling of the other. Traditionalists maintain that *stanch* is the verb meaning "to stop the flow of" <A tourniquet will *stanch* the blood> and *staunch* is the adjective meaning "sturdy, true, or faithful" <A *staunch* friend would come to your aid at a time like this>. But since both spellings are accepted for either sense, confusion about which word to use when is unnecessary

starboard/port *see* **port**

state/say *State* and *say* can be used interchangeably to mean "to express in words." *State,* however, carries the connotation of expressing the details about something <I tried to *state* my case, but the judge told me to sit down and be quiet>, while *say* can be used for any sort of verbal expression <I wanted to *say* what I felt> and even for what is shown <The clock *says* a quarter to four>

stationary/stationery *Stationary* is an adjective meaning "still, not moving" <a *stationary* bike>. *Stationery* is a noun meaning "writing materials" <She wanted to send us a letter, but she didn't have any *stationery* in the house>. *Stationery* is what's sold by a *stationer,* one who has a permanent location or *station* for selling books or related materials; this history of the word may help keep it from being confused with *stationary*

stigma/stigmata A *stigma* is "a mark, stain, or spot," either figurative or actual <He suffered the *stigma* of his association with the Communist party>. *Stigmata* is the plural of *stigma* (the plural can also be *stigmas),* but it is most often used to mean "marks like those left on Christ's crucified body" <a holy shroud showing the *stigmata*>

stink/odor/smell *see* **odor**

strait/straight Although it might be tempting to assume that *strait* is a simplified spelling of *straight,* much as *lite* has come to substitute for *light,* these are two very different words with very different meanings. A *strait* is either "a narrow waterway connecting two larger bodies of water" <the *Strait* of Magellan> or "a difficulty," usually used in the plural <His penny-wise attitude is going to put us in dire *straits*>. *Straight* means "uncurved" <Go *straight* down the road>, "tidy or orderly" <Try to get this place *straight*>, "clear and straightforward" <Let me get this *straight,* you want me to pick him up?>, "not homosexual" <He resisted the man's advances, protesting that he was *straight*>, "without additions or dilution" <Give her a *straight* whisky>, or in poker "five cards in numerical order" <I'm holding a *straight,* ten high> *see* **bay/gulf/strait/sound**

strategy/tactics A *strategy* is "a large-scale plan of action" for military or other purposes <The manager's *strategy* is simple: We will try to win more games than any other team, thereby assuring us of playing in the championships>. A *strategy* outlines a number of objectives that must be met to make it work. And in order to meet those objectives, planners develop *tactics,* "plans for each specific aspect of an overall plan" <The manager needs to decide which *tactics* he wants to use in this situation, whether to bring his outfielders in or attempt a decoy play that might catch the base runner unawares>

stream/creek/brook/river/kill *see* **kill**

street/avenue/road *see* **road**

stress/strain In the sense "tension resulting from mental, physical, or emotional overexertion" <I'm under a lot of *stress* trying to finish this book on time> and the broader sense "pressure" <The *strain* our belongings are putting on the floor is more noticeable now that the supporting beams have been removed>, *stress* and *strain* are synonymous. The phrase *stress and strain* is redundant and should be avoided except in instances where pressure needs to be greatly emphasized

stringed/strung *Stringed* is an adjective that means "having strings" <The guitar is a *stringed* instrument> or "produced by strings" <the *stringed* cacophony of an orchestra tuning up>; it does not serve as the past tense of *string,* which is *strung* <He was *strung* up at dawn>

student/pupil *see* **pupil**

style/élan *see* **élan**

substantial/substantive These words are interchangeable, meaning "having substance or reality" <She's waiting for the rumors to turn into a *substantial* offer>, "ample or considerable" <a *substantive* amount of money>, "basic or essential" <There's little *substantial* difference between the two words>, or "sturdy" <a *substantive* little hut that will keep out the elements> *see* **essentially/substantially**

substitute/substitution In the sense "someone or something that takes the place of another," *substitute* and *substitution* are synonyms <Here's my *substitute,* and that guy is your *substitution*>, although *substitute* is more commonly used. *Substitution* is more frequently used to mean "an act of replacement" <Coach said she'd make a *substitution* after this round>

sunk/sank *see* **sank**

supine/prone *see* **prone**

supper/dinner *see* **dinner**

survive/endure *see* **endure**

swam/swum The regular past tense of *swim* is *swam* <She *swam* across the pool twenty-five times every day>. *Swum* is now considered unacceptable in this tense unless it is acting as a past participle or passive verb <The English Channel has been *swum* time and again, but never easily>

sympathy/empathy *see* **empathy**

synonym/homonym *see* **homonym**

T

tactics/strategy *see* **strategy**

take/bring *see* **bring**

talk to/talk with There is a subtle difference in meaning between these two phrases. To *talk to* means "to address" in a one-sided discourse wherein one person does all the talking <The captain *talked to* the crew about their lack of discipline>. To *talk with* means "to converse together" in a mutual exchange in which both sides participate <The captain *talked with* the crew about ways to improve discipline>. *Talk with* is sometimes also used to mean "to address" <Mom is definitely going to *talk with* my sister about this mess>, and although this use implies at least some limited opportunity for response, it does not suggest a reciprocal exchange

tap/bug Both *tap* and *bug* are used to mean "a surreptitious listening device," but they differ in the placement of that device. A *tap* is placed on a telephone line to listen to phone conversations, and a *bug* is placed in a room to listen to whatever goes on there

tart/pie *Tart* and *pie* both mean "a pastry shell filled with fruit or custard," but a *tart* is smaller than a *pie.* A *pie* could contain meat and vegetables instead of fruit or custard <a chicken *pie*>, and with such filling would be a *pie* regardless of its size

tasty/tasteful These adjectives have to do with different senses of *taste,* and although they are often used one for the other in informal contexts, the careful writer will differentiate between them. *Tasty* means "flavorful" <a *tasty* plate of spareribs and black-eyed peas> and, by extension, "attractive or interesting" <The best thing about her parties is that she dishes up some *tasty* scuttlebutt about the TV industry>. *Tasteful* means "exhibiting good esthetic judgment" <a *tasteful* film that doesn't show rapes or murders in graphic detail>

taunt/taught To *taunt* means "to insult or challenge" <The schoolyard bullies *taunted* him about his new haircut>. *Taught* is the past tense of *teach,* "to educate or make known" <We were *taught* not to make fun of others>

taut/taught Although they sound the same, *taut* and *taught* are very different in meaning. *Taut* is an adjective meaning "stretched tight" <Make sure that rope is *taut* so the ship won't move about>. *Taught,* the past tense of *teach,* means "to educate or make known" <The sailor *taught* us how to tie knots that won't slip>

tax/duty *see* **duty**

telegraph/telegram A *telegraph* is "a system of communicating messages electrically, usually between stations connected by wires" <Before the invention of the telephone, the *telegraph* was the fastest way to transmit messages> or "a message transmitted in this way." In this second sense, *telegraph* is synonymous with *telegram* <She got a *telegram* congratulating her on her promotion>

terrain/ground In the sense "a specific piece of land," *terrain* and *ground* can be used interchangeably. But *terrain* usually refers to "the geography or physical features of a piece of land" <the rocky *terrain* along the coast of Maine>, a meaning the more general *ground* doesn't cover

that/if *see* **if**

that/which These pronouns are used to introduce a clause that elaborates on the subject of a sentence. They are differentiated on the basis of whether the subject is a person or not, and on whether the clause is essential to the meaning of the sentence or not. *That* can be used to introduce a clause having to do with people, things, or animals; *which* is employed for nonhuman subjects. *That* is used with what are known as restrictive clauses, clauses without which the sentence won't make sense or won't have the same meaning <Grammar is a subject *that* cannot be understood without a grasp of the language> <You are the one person *that* I don't understand>; in some sentences, like the second example given here, *that* can be left out altogether, but if a pronoun is used, *that* is the right one to choose. *Which* introduces nonrestrictive clauses, clauses that add meaning to a sentence but aren't essential; these clauses are usually set off with commas and could be enclosed in parentheses <The computer, *which* isn't working, is on the desk>. This example could be rewritten as "The computer is on the desk, but it isn't working"; if *that* were used instead of *which,* the sentence would mean "The nonfunctioning computer (as opposed to any other computers around) is on the desk." The distinction between *which* and *that* is a very difficult one to figure out in many cases. The best way to decide which to choose is to try eliminating the clause being introduced. If the sentence has the same basic meaning without the clause <The computer is on the desk>, *which* should introduce it; if the meaning is quite different without the clause <Grammar is a subject>, *that* should introduce it

that/who *That* and *who* are used as pronouns to introduce clauses that have people as their subjects. The difference between them is not whether the subject is human or not, but whether the clause is restrictive (essential) or nonrestrictive (incidental). *That,* as described in the entry *that/which,* is used with restrictive clauses <The people *that* are angry should get mad at the mayor, not at me>. *Who* is employed at the beginning of nonrestrictive clauses <The people, *who* are angry, should get mad at the mayor, not at me>. The first example is about those people who are angry, the second about an undefined mass of people or all people. As described in the entry *that/which,* try removing the clause to see whether *that* or *who* is appropriate

theft/robbery/burglary/larceny *see* **burglary**

their/his/his or her *see* **everyone . . . his**

thirdly/third As with *first/firstly* and *second/secondly,* either *third* or *thirdly* is correct as an adverb meaning "in the third place." But *thirdly* is very cumbersome when enumerating points because it requires the use of *firstly* to maintain consistency, and *firstly* sounds ridiculous. Use *first, second,* and *third* <We need a new home because, first, our house is too small, second, our neighborhood is lousy, and *third,* it's time for a change>

though/although As conjunctions meaning "despite the fact that," "however," or "even if," *though* and *although* are interchangeable <I'm coming over, *although* I have a cold> <*Though* there might be ten feet of snow on the ground, she'll get there>

thrash/thresh *Thrash* originated as a variant spelling of *thresh,* and although they are sometimes used interchangeably they have each developed a basic meaning that should be distinguished from the other's. *Thrash* means "to beat or flog a person" <My dad could *thrash* your dad> and, by extension, "to utterly defeat or trounce" <The Bulldogs were *thrashed* yet again, this time by the Crimsons>. *Thresh* means "to separate seeds from straw by beating." Either *thresh* or *thrash* can be used with *over* to mean "to go over repeatedly" <We *threshed* (or *thrashed)* the problem over all night without reaching a solution>

thus/thusly The adverb meaning "as stated," "so," or "consequently" is *thus. Thusly* is sometimes used either for humorous effect or because of the confused notion that all adverbs must end in *ly,* but it is not acceptable in standard English

tight/tightly *Tight* is the adjective meaning "closely set" or "securely attached." For the adverbial form, either *tight* or *tightly* is correct <Hold on *tight*> <fasten *tightly*>

till/until *Till* and *until* are interchangeable whether used as a preposition <He'll be gone *till* the end of the month> or a conjunction <She kept working *until* she dropped dead at her desk>

tint/color/hue *see* **hue**

title/entitle *see* **entitle**

to/too/two If the difference between these words wasn't learned in elementary school, it's probably too late to learn it now. But for what it's worth, *to* serves as a preposition <My momma sent me *to* the store> or as an adverb <When he came *to,* all the money was gone>; *too* means "also" <She ordered a steak with potatoes and peas, and a salad *too*>; and *two* is "the cardinal number between one and three" <I wanted *two* wives but the law only permitted me to have one>

tornado/cyclone A *tornado* is "a windstorm with a funnel-shaped cloud" and a *cyclone* is "a rapidly circulating windstorm centered around low pressure," but for those who are not meteorologists, the words can be used interchangeably to mean "a violent windstorm of any sort"

tortuous/torturous Although related, *tortuous* and *torturous* are used quite differently. *Tortuous* means "crooked" in the senses "winding, twisted" <a *tortuous* road> or "deceitful, tricky" <Tricky Dick was a *tortuous* politician>. *Torturous* is the adjective form of *torture,* meaning "painful" <That was a *torturous* meeting for him, getting berated in front of the entire board of trustees>

toward/towards In all senses, *toward* and *towards* can be used interchangeably <She's headed *toward* home> <Kissinger's efforts *towards* peace in the Middle East>. *Toward* is generally preferred in the U.S.

transient/transitory Both *transient* and *transitory* mean "having a brief or temporary existence," but they are applied to different subjects. *Transient* is used mostly to describe people who are present for a short time or the places they stay <*transient* labor> <a *transient* hotel>. *Transitory* is applied primarily to things or events that are by their very nature temporary or short-lived <Peace in Northern Ireland tends to be a *transitory* condition>

transpire/happen Arbiters of correct usage disagree vehemently about whether *transpire* can be used synonymously with *happen* to mean "to occur." It was accepted in this sense by Noah Webster in his 1826 dictionary, but is rejected as a misuse by the *Oxford English Dictionary.* To avoid the slings and arrows of pedants, use *happen* to mean "to occur" and keep *transpire* for the sense "to become known despite efforts to keep secret" <Our carefully concealed plans were *transpired* to the press>

trash/debris/garbage *see* **debris**

treachery/treason These terms both mean "a betrayal," but they are used for different sorts of betrayals. *Treachery* is "a betrayal of a confidence" <Telling my husband what I told you was an act of *treachery*>. *Treason* is "a betrayal of one's country" <Telling the Bulgarians what your president told you was an act of *treason*>

tread/trod/treaded/trodden *Tread* is the present-tense form of the verb meaning "to walk on" <When I

walk the city streets I *tread* on the path of history>. The past tense in the active voice is *trod* or *treaded* <She had *trod* this path before>; in the passive voice, use *trodden* or *trod* <a quiet country lane that had not been *trodden* in recent times>

trick/gimmick *see* **gimmick**

triumvirate/trio In the sense "an association of three people," *triumvirate* and *trio* are interchangeable <Our panel today is being led by a distinguished *triumvirate,* the partners in the law firm Dewey, Gypum, & Howe>. Both words stress the association of the three people being described and cannot be properly used to mean simply "three people"

troop/troupe A *troop* is "a group of people" of any sort <Boy Scout *troop*>. A *troupe* is "a group of actors, singers, or dancers" <The Bolshoi *troupe* will be coming to Washington in the spring>

try/endeavor *see* **endeavor**

try to/try and In formal writing, the correct phrase is *try to* <I'm going to *try to* find out who's in charge here>. In less formal writing or in speech, *try and* is considered an acceptable substitute <Yvonne said she'd *try and* get through to us this afternoon>

turtle/tortoise A *turtle* is "a land, freshwater, or marine reptile that carries a shell." A *tortoise* is mostly used to mean "a land turtle," which is why a *tortoise* raced with a hare in the classic children's story. *Tortoise* is the word used to mean "a slow person" <Ron Hassey can hit and catch, but he's something of a *tortoise* on the base paths>

two/to/too *see* **to**

typhoon/hurricane/gale A *typhoon* is "a severe tropical windstorm occurring in the western Pacific Ocean or China Sea." A *hurricane* is "a severe tropical windstorm" that can occur in many places in the world. In the U.S. there are *hurricanes;* in the Philippines, an identical storm is a *typhoon.* A *gale* can occur anywhere in the world; it's "a strong wind" or, meteorologically speaking, "a wind of between thirty-two and sixty-three miles per hour"

unalienable/inalienable *see* **inalienable**

unattached/detached *Unattached* usually applies to people or things and to a lesser extent is used to describe buildings and property; it can mean "not married" <an *unattached* man in his late thirties> or "not seized in legal proceedings" <His free-lance income is the only thing left *unattached* in the settlement>, or "not connected" <The Siamese twins were *unattached* except at the hands>. *Detached* is most often applied to physical property <a *detached* home>, but when used to describe people it means "indifferent, aloof" <That *detached* attitude won't get you anywhere in this commune>

unartistic/inartistic Both words mean "not artistic," but they apply somewhat differently. *Unartistic* is mostly used to mean "not inclined to create art" <He goes to painting class three times a week, but he's really *unartistic*

and it shows in what he paints>. *Inartistic* can apply to works of art in the sense "not considered to be art" <Her *inartistic* doodlings aren't worth the paper they're drawn on> or to people in the sense "not understanding of art" <I can tell if I like it or not, but I'm basically *inartistic*>

unaware/unawares The adjective meaning "not aware" is *unaware* <We were *unaware* of her present circumstances>. Either *unaware* or *unawares* can be used for the adverb meaning "unexpectedly, by surprise" <He was suddenly standing in my bedroom, catching me quite *unawares*> *see* **oblivious/unaware**

under/below *see* **below**

underlay/underlie *Underlay* means "to raise or support by something laid under," and applies only to tangible things <Styrofoam *underlays* the rocks and concrete used to make the sidewalk>. *Underlie* applies to theories or beliefs in the sense "to support" <Marxist doctrine *underlies* their terrorist activities>. The words are not interchangeable

understand/construe *see* **construe**

undertaker/funeral director/mortician *see* **funeral director**

undertone/overtone *see* **overtone**

undiscriminating/indiscriminate *see* **indiscriminate**

undoubtedly/doubtless *see* **doubtless**

undulate/ripple To *undulate* means "to move in smooth waves"; the waves can be small or large <The

water in the pool *undulated* for several minutes after he dived in>. To *ripple* means "to move in small waves" <Pebbles made the water *ripple*>

uneatable/inedible Both words apply to food that isn't fit to be eaten, but the reason it shouldn't be eaten is different for each. *Uneatable* means "unfit to be eaten because of its condition" <We left the salmon steaks on the grill for so long they were *uneatable*>. *Inedible* means "unfit to be eaten because of its nature" <Poisonous mushrooms are *inedible*>. However, this distinction is often ignored

unexceptionable/unacceptable *Unexceptionable* means "without discernible fault," something to which exception cannot be taken <Being hit by a car is an *unexceptionable* excuse for not having your work done>. *Unacceptable* is just the opposite, meaning "not pleasing or acceptable" <Oversleeping is an *unacceptable* excuse for not having your work done>

unilateral/multilateral/bilateral *see* **bilateral**

uninterested/disinterested *see* **disinterested**

unique/unusual/special *Unique* is used by careful writers and speakers to mean "singular, one of a kind"; it applies to things that are unlike any others, and should not be modified by words like *most, rather,* or *somewhat* <Traveling in outer space is a *unique* experience>. *Unusual* means "out of the ordinary" and describes things that aren't like those that happen regularly; it can be modified to show how irregular something is <Meeting the president is an *unusual* event for people like me>. *Special* also means "out of the ordinary," but it is usually applied to people, things, or events that are unusual in a positive sense <Giving him a surprise party was a *special* way of showing how much she cares for him>

university/college *see* **college**

unloose/unloosen/loosen *see* **loosen**

unprecedented/rare This pair is akin to *unique* and *unusual. Unprecedented* means "without precedent" and applies to things the likes of which have not been seen before <Hitting four home runs in a single game is an *unprecedented* event in this league>. *Rare* means "uncommon, unusual"; it's used to describe things that don't ordinarily happen <Hitting a single home run is a *rare* event for me>

unravel/ravel *see* **ravel**

unreadable/illegible *see* **illegible**

until/till *see* **till**

upon/on *Upon* and *on* are interchangeable prepositions indicating the position of one thing relative to another. *Upon* can be used to indicate motion <She jumped *upon* a chair and began exhorting the crowd> and *on* to indicate rest <The cup rested *on* the coaster>, but this differentiation is not absolute and is frequently ignored, even by careful writers

upward/upwards *Upwards* is acceptable in any of the adverbial senses for which *upward* can be used

us/we *Us* and *we* are both pronouns that refer to two or more people. *Us* is used when the people being referred to are the object of the verb <Are you talking to

us?> or preposition <Some of *us* peons like to have at least one day off a week>. *We* comes into play as the subject of the verb <*We* are not amused>. Confusion often arises when a pronoun is needed before a noun, as in the second example of *us* above. One way to decide which to use is to eliminate the noun and see if the phrase sounds right; "some of *we*" is obviously wrong, making the correct choice "some of *us*"

usage/use *Usage* and *use* both mean "the act of utilizing, employing, or applying something." But *usage* is appropriate when referring to "a set of rules or the accepted procedures governing how something is utilized" <Correct *usage* of the language will be easier if you refer to this book> or "the manner in which something is employed" <Lack of maintenance can limit the *usage* of a car>. *Use* can be employed in these senses, too, but it is a more general term that applies to any sort of utilization or application <*Use* of the telephone is restricted to local calls>. *Usage* is often misused in an effort to sound more learned; in most cases, *use* would be the better choice

use/utilize *Use,* the verb, is employed in more general senses, much like *use,* the noun. It implies the implementation of something to achieve a result <I *use* a spoon to eat porridge>. *Utilize* is more specifically applied to something employed in a new or practical fashion, senses for which *use* can also be used <*Utilize* your time to your own advantage>. *Utilize* is frequently misused to make a plain sentence sound more important, but if there is any doubt, *use* is the correct choice

U.S.S.R./Russia *see* **Russia**

venial/venal *Venial* is usually applied to sins; it means "forgivable" <The priest absolved her for telling white lies, saying they were *venial* sins>. *Venal* has to do with evil of another sort; it means "corruptible" <Cops in this precinct have a reputation for being the most *venal* cops in the city> or "purchasable" <The rights to this tract of land are *venal*>

venturous/venturesome/adventurous/adventuresome *see* **adventurous**

verbal/oral *see* **oral**

viable/workable/possible Each of these words has distinct meanings for which it can be used. *Viable* means "capable of continued life or existence" <A fetus is usually not *viable* until it has gestated for seven months> or "likely to have continued effectiveness" <a more *viable*

agreement than the last one>. *Workable* is applied to plans or ideas in the sense "likely to be successful" <Employee management is a *workable* approach to keeping the factory open>. *Possible* means "having the potential to be achieved"; it is used to describe the relative likelihood that something can be done <It's *possible* she could be convinced to accept the award>

violin/fiddle *see* **fiddle**

viral/virile *Viral* means "having to do with a virus" <a *viral* infection>. *Virile* means "manly" <a *virile* group of weightlifters>. The words are not interchangeable

virtually/practically These words, once neatly distinguished from each other, have become virtually synonymous. In the sense "almost," *virtually* and *practically* are interchangeable <I've *virtually* finished writing this book> <We're *practically* home>. *Practically* is the better choice for the sense "for all practical purposes" <a usage guide that *practically* replaces all others>, although *virtually* can be used in this way too

visible/visual Either *visible* or *visual* can be used to mean "able to be seen," "noticeable," although *visible* is more common in these senses. *Visual* is the right choice for the meaning "having to do with sight" <That painting is a *visual* delight>

vitae/resume *see* **resume**

vulgar/obscene/profane *see* **obscene**

warm/warmly In most cases, *warm* is an adjective <a *warm* sensation> and *warmly* an adverb <bundle up *warmly*>. When preceded by the word *feel,* however, care must be taken about the sense of *warm* being indicated: If talking about temperature, use *warm* <I feel *warm* in this overheated house>; if the subject is affection, use *warmly* <He feels *warmly* about his stay here>

warp/woof Knitters need to know their *warp* from their *woof. Warp* is "a number of yarns strung lengthwise on a loom." *Woof* is "yarn threaded between the warp"

we/us *see* **us**

well/good *see* **good**

wharf/dock/jetty/pier *see* **dock**

whence Rarely used in modern American English, *whence* is a word that is frequently misused when it does appear. It means "from where" and therefore should not be used with *from* <He wondered *whence* she came>

whether/if Both terms introduce conditional clauses, but the nature of those clauses determines which word is more appropriate. When alternatives are being raised, *whether* is the better choice <We can't decide *whether* to go to your party or Paul's>. When only one of the possibilities is being mentioned, *if* is more often used <She doesn't know *if* she should be here>, although either word can be used

whether/whether or not Many uses of *whether* imply an *or not* <I can't decide *whether* to go out today>; the *or not* can be included or left out, depending on the writer's own sense of euphony

which/that *see* **that**

whither *Whither* is another word that's rarely used but frequently misused when it does appear (see *whence).* It means "to what place" and therefore does not need the word *to* <*Whither* are you going?>

who/whom Perhaps the most difficult decision a careful writer or speaker must make is when to use *who* and when to use *whom.* The problem is so perplexing that for more than a hundred years, wordsmiths have predicted (and no doubt hoped for) the demise of the word *whom.* To a small extent, this prediction has come true: *whom* is nearly extinct in spoken American English and can be ignored in informal writing. But those contexts that demand correct, formal language require the proper use of *whom.* In questions where the pronoun is the object of a verb or preposition, *whom* is the correct choice

<*Whom* did you say was calling?> <To *whom* am I speaking?>. Indirect questions using the pronoun as the object of a verb or preposition also require *whom* <She wants to know *whom* she should see about a job>. It is often easy to mistake the subject of a clause for the object of a verb; if the clause can stand alone and has a subject, verb, and object, and the sentence's verb is followed by an object that's not part of the clause, the subject of the clause should be *who,* not *whom* <He talked to a musician *who* he thought would make an excellent addition to his band>

whoever/whomever *Whoever* and *whomever* follow the same rules as *who* and *whom* (see the preceding entry)

whole/hole *see* **hole**

wide/broad *see* **broad**

will/shall *see* **shall**

winsome/winning *Winsome* and *winning* both mean "pleasing and delightful," but they apply to people in different ways. *Winsome* is usually said of a person and carries the implication of childlike innocence <He's a *winsome* fellow not given to talking business unless he has to>. *Winning* is mostly used to describe one aspect of a person <a *winning* smile> <a *winning* personality>

within/in In the sense "inside," *within* and *in* can be synonyms <I do all my work *within* the house> <I also do much of my entertaining *in* the house>. But *within* usually has the meaning "up to but not beyond the limits of" <*within* these four walls> <*within* an hour>, while *in* is used for "contained by" <squirrels *in* these four walls> or "at the point of" <*in* an hour>

without/outside As an adverb meaning "from an external perspective," either *without* or *outside* is acceptable <She views her neighbor's home only from *without*> <He stands *outside* waiting to be asked in>

with regard to/as regards/in regard to *see* **in regard to**

woman/female *see* **female**

woman/lady *see* **lady**

wood/wooden *Wood* and *wooden* can be used interchangeably as adjectives meaning "made of wood" <a *wood* box> <a *wooden* spoon>. The sense "stiff, expressionless" is represented by *wooden* <a *wooden* kind of person who seems uncomfortable no matter where she is>

woolen/woolly *Woolen* means "made of wool" <a *woolen* scarf>. *Woolly* can be used in this sense, too, although it also means "covered with wool" <a *woolly* sheep>, "fuzzy in thought or speech" <Nick Charles doesn't seem *woolly* no matter how many martinis he has>, or "boisterous and unrestrained" <the wild and *woolly* establishments in this town>

workable/possible/viable *see* **viable**

would/should *see* **should**

woven/wove/weaved The past tense of *weave* "to interlace yarn" can be either *wove* or *weaved* in the active voice <He *wove* a beautiful Kente cloth> <She *weaved* all night trying to finish the piece>. In the passive voice, *woven* or *weaved* is correct <This fabric was *woven* from gold threads>. The past tense of *weave,* "to move unsteadily from side to side," is *weaved* <The car *weaved* all over the road>

wrack/rack *see* **rack**

wrapped/wrapt/rapt *see* **rapt**

write/author *see* **author**

write/wright/right/rite *see* **right**

X Y Z

Xerox/photocopy/copy Despite widespread use as a generic term, *Xerox* is a trademark that applies only to copies made on a machine produced by the Xerox Corporation. The general term for a copy of graphic material made on a machine that uses a photographic process is *photocopy.* A *copy* can be made in any of several ways, including photocopying or the use of carbon paper

X-rayed/X-rated Something that's been *X-rayed* has been "photographed or treated with a specific type of radiation that penetrates the outer surface to show what's underneath." Something that's been *X-rated* has been "deemed suitable only for adults," especially films, books, or magazines that are sexually explicit

yea/yeah *Yea* means "yes," and is used in voting orally <When the role is called, cast your vote by saying *yea* or nay>. It is also used as an interjection meaning "hurrah" <*Yea!* Our team won!>, in which sense it is sometimes spelled *yay.* As an adverb it can mean "to this extent" <She caught a fish that was *yea* big>. *Yeah* means "yes," but it is used in conversation, not in voting <*Yeah,* I guess I'll have another piece of pie>

your/you're *Your* is the adjective meaning "of or belonging to you" <Is this *your* coat?>. *You're* is a contraction of "you are" <*You're* going to the dance on Saturday>. Despite the apostrophe, a telltale sign of a contraction, many writers still confuse the two words

zip/ZIP The lowercase *zip* is a slang term that can be used to mean "vitality" <He just doesn't seem to have much *zip* anymore> or "zero, nothing" <She went in looking for a raise and came out with *zip*>. The postal delivery number that appears at the end of a U.S. address is known as the ZIP code or ZIP, which stands for *z*one *i*mprovement *p*lan; it is usually styled in all capital letters <I can never remember my ZIP>